Dawn Jagger is a community care worker and reiki practitioner. Reiki is an ancient form of energy healing. Dawn is a mother of two (her daughter is deceased) and a grandmother of eleven, her eldest grandchild is twenty-years-old. He has a rare medical condition.

This book is written in memory of my late daughter, Claire.

Dawn Jagger

FROM CHAOS TO ORDER

AUSTIN MACAULEY PUBLISHERS™
LONDON • CAMBRIDGE • NEW YORK • SHARJAH

All of the events in this memoir are true to the best of author's memory. The views expressed in this memoir are solely those of the author.

A CIP catalogue record for this title is available from the British Library.

ISBN 9781528988247 (Paperback)
ISBN 9781528988254 (ePub e-book)

www.austinmacauley.com

First Published 2021
Austin Macauley Publishers Ltd
1 Canada Square
Canary Wharf
London
E14 5AA

I would like to thank my family and friends for their continued support and belief in me and of my belief in the unknown, Oprah Winfrey for her weekly programme, Super Soul Sunday and Joyce Meyer for her daily programme, Living Everyday Life.

Table of Contents

(1)
True Experience, Of Communication with Spirit World

November 1996

I was going through a difficult time in my marriage; to give us space, I rented a house. My son, Andy, stayed with his dad while my daughter, Claire, came with me. Both Andy and Claire seemed happy with this arrangement. I worked part-time and had a keen interest in fitness; I loved cycling. Friday and Sunday evenings, I went out for a drink with friends. Andy and Claire were popular teenagers, now doing their own thing. I felt I had let go of responsibility to a certain extent. The house we rented was very clean, comfortable and fully furnished; it had a lovely homely feel.

One night, I was woken up by the sound of a piano playing. I lifted my head off the pillow and it stopped playing. I fell back to sleep. This started happening most nights and every time I would lift my head off the pillow, it would immediately stop playing. I decided to try and stay awake, hoping it would start to play, to prove to myself that I wasn't dreaming. It never did; I did notice something moving on the bed, it was as if a cat was pawing at the quilt. If it was the early hours and coming light, I would gently lift my head up to see if I could see anything. I couldn't but could still feel the movement. The next day, I would go to work, quite excited, to tell my friends that I had a cat ghost who plonks away on the piano. There was never a tune; just random notes being played. There were lots of comments at work, but all harmless fun. I'm not sure, even now, what my friends really thought. Maybe because Claire lived with me, they thought Claire was plonking away on the piano in the middle of the night. This was not so. Things had gotten more intense as the weeks went by. While I would lie awake, I could feel the bed vibrating very fast. I would get out of bed and kneel down with my hands on the bed. I could feel the vibration but could see no movement at all. The toilet roll holder would spin through the night. I would expect the paper to be in a pile the next morning, but it never was. Some mornings, I would get up and there would be broken curtain hooks on the floor. In the living room and in the bedroom, where the piano was, the curtains were hanging as if someone had been swinging on them. Claire had not been swinging on the curtains, playing the piano or spinning the toilet roll holder; she was fast asleep in her bed. She certainly wasn't making my bed vibrate or moving on it while I was sleeping. I was absolutely fascinated, I thought of films like 'Ghost' and my all-time favourite as a child, 'Scrooge'. They were based on fact; there was definitely more than Claire and me, in this house.

One night, I had someone staying over. We had just gone to bed when the toilet roll holder began to spin. It had only done this while I was sleeping, waking me up, but now I was wide-awake. I had already told my friend about all the things that were happening; now at last, someone else has heard this. My friend said it would be wind in the drainpipes, but how could he explain what happened next? Footsteps walked along the landing and knocked at the door three times. I quickly got out of bed and opened the door. There was no one there and Claire's door was closed. There was no way she could have hurried back to her room and closed her door without us hearing her. My friend left the next morning, asking me not to tell anyone; I don't think he could handle someone's jokes. It didn't matter to me what anyone said; I felt so lucky to be having this experience. I noticed that if I got up to go to the toilet in the night, I could feel a strong presence even if I couldn't see anything. Until this particular night, I had not felt scared or threatened by whatever this was. However, this night there was a bright and dazzling light coming from the bedroom where the piano was; there was also a loud humming sound. I knelt by the bed that I was sleeping in; it was vibrating so fast, the whole house seemed alive with sound, light and vibration. I now had a mixture of fascination and fear; I felt I needed answers. Another night, when woken by movement on the bed, I felt a strange feeling. Working its way from my feet, up my calves, I felt like I was floating up in the corner of the bedroom. Yet, I was fully aware and I knew I was in my bed. I had a strange sensation in my mouth; my tongue felt swollen and spongy. Claire was sleeping in bed with me but stayed fast asleep; whatever was happening to me was not affecting Claire. I was really frightened; I jumped out of bed and rushed downstairs to phone the Samaritans help line, why them, I'm not sure, I felt I was in a desperate situation out of my control, I must have sounded crazy when

I told them what was happening in the house. They told me I should maybe call a priest. I was exhausted; I went back to bed. I must have fallen straight to sleep, with nothing else happening that night. The next time I was woken by the sound of the piano, we got a taxi to my sister Audra's house. We just got settled in bed when I could hear that damn piano playing, my sister Audra doesn't have a piano so how was this possible? I still do not know if Claire experienced any of these things. My friend, Fiona, who rented the house before me, said she saw a woman in the house, twice; her daughter also experienced some of the things that I experienced. My landlord rang me one day, telling me his house had sold and asking me to find alternative accommodation. These are the events of my last week living there.

MONDAY. My friends, Janine and Angie, brought a lovely young girl, Vanessa to see me, she is a spiritualist, They must have been concerned about my mental state, due to the fact that all I was focusing on was the activity in the house. What a relief when at last, she explained that there was a spirit trying to communicate with me. She told me exactly what to do the next time I felt a presence. Telling me that within three days I would become aware of who this spirit was and what they needed me to do in order for them to rest in peace. This brought back my fascination, instead of the fear, that had taken over.

TUESDAY. I don't recall anything.

WEDNESDAY. I came home from work, the piano playing as I unlocked the door, very unusual for this time of day. I walked up to the bedroom; it had stopped by the time I got up there. I went in; the room seemed bright but not the dazzling brightness like that night. The room had a misty, icy feel. I did and said what the spiritualist Vanessa told me, then left the room. I don't recall anything else happening that night.

THURSDAY. Claire was ill so I made her comfortable, leaving the phone by her bed and telling her to ring me at work if she needed anything. I hadn't been at work long when I felt unwell. My legs felt like lead; my head felt fuzzy and I was lightheaded as if I could pass out. I went to phone Claire, she didn't answer. I got on my bike, cycled home, ran to Claire's room asking why she didn't answer the phone. She said it never rang. I then realised that I was perfectly well and must have been okay while cycling home. I then remembered what Vanessa had said, about following my intuition. I felt the need to talk to the next-door neighbour. I had no idea what I was going to say; I had never spoken to the neighbours, but now the urge was strong. I knocked at the door and a lady answered, I just blurted out all the things that had been happening. This lady told me she had been very good friends with the lady whose house I was living in. She told me they had been left baffled by her wishes for a non-religious burial, because she had been a religious lady. This is something I now feel I understand but it meant nothing to me at the time. I was moving out of the rented house the next day, so I thanked this lady for her time and left. When I got in I put the kettle on, there was a knock at the door it was the lady from next door, she asked if I would like help moving out, and because the kettle was boiling I offered her a coffee. She said no thanks and she went on to tell me the lady whose house I was living in always had the kettle on. She loved her cups of tea. I then realised the number of times I'd gone to make a cup of coffee; it was as if someone had knocked my elbow, knocking coffee all over the worktop. Just another way of confirming who this spirit was. I walked with my neighbour down the drive; we stood talking. I noticed a lump, pulsing just at the bottom of my ribs at my left side; you could see that it was slightly swollen in this area. I asked what the lady's illness had been, she told me what this lady had passed away with, she then described how the illness had affected her. she said her left side of her upper body was swollen and also that her legs had felt like lead, but she still wanted to walk down her drive to the ambulance. How strange, my legs had felt like lead earlier in the day. How is it possible for someone, no longer alive, to impress on my body something she experienced before passing?

I went back into the house and switched the kettle back on. I got some washing to hang out; as I walked towards the door, a small metal object was vibrating in mid-air, just above my eye level. It had not fallen from anywhere; it was just hovering. It then fell to the floor, there was no breeze and it was metal so it could not just float. Then, as it had done many times before, the electricity went off. I pressed the fuse switch; it would not stay pressed; when I took my finger off, it just flicked back. I phoned my friend who told me what to do. I said, "I've done it many times before, it will not stay on." He reluctantly came and when he pressed the switch, it stayed on. He looked at me asking if I was okay. I was far from okay, I was feeling quite stressed now. It had been a strange day, lots of unusual things happening. I showed Alan the object; he told me it was a speaker connection. I thought he was wrong, telling him it must be something to do with the kettle; I'd just put the kettle on before the electricity went off. He left, looking quite concerned about me. Looking back, I think many people were worried about my state of mind. Luckily, they knew that I was not seeking attention or telling lies. Some have since had their own experiences. I now needed to know what this object was; it was quite obvious it would lead me to something connected to all this activity. I went into town, to a spare parts shop and they confirmed as Alan had said. It was a speaker connection. I was totally baffled, what did it mean? I felt I needed to speak to my landlord and tell him what had been happening in his house. I rang him; he said he would call on his way home from work. I told him everything, also showing him the metal object. I now had to accept it was a speaker connection, he said that his mother had replaced them. This had been in a cabinet in the dining room. He went on to say that his family had experienced something like this before. He told me he would stay in the house before the new owners moved in. This made sense to me. I felt I had done what his mum needed me to do.

FRIDAY. My landlord called for his keys and I could sense his mum behind my right shoulder. I knew that he couldn't sense her, I didn't say anything to him. We moved back into our family home.

FRIDAY NIGHT. I went to bed and I was just dropping off to sleep when the piano started playing. How was this possible, when I didn't have a piano? I did eventually fall asleep.

SATURDAY NIGHT. That damn piano. As soon as I got settled in bed, it started to play. It was about eleven thirty p.m. but I got up and phoned my landlord. I said, "You haven't stayed at your house have you?"

He said no he hadn't. I asked if he would go and stay, telling him about the piano playing and he said he would. I went back to bed, straight to sleep, with nothing else happening.

TUESDAY. I got a call from my landlord, asking how I was. I told him that nothing else had happened since I spoke with him on Saturday night. He said that he and his brother stayed at the house on Sunday, until midnight, but didn't experience anything. I felt that I had done what his mum wanted. I believe she got peace from knowing her sons believed in her presence, enough to go back to their family home.

Bible… Mark .9.9…Rise from death

My interpretation ……

Our energy body (Aura) continues to survive when our physical body dies. The aura rises, releases from our physical body.

It is now 2017. I have a clear understanding of how our communication with the spirit world works. We not only have a physical body, but we also have an energy body (aura /spiritual body). This energy body is invisible unless you have auric vision. This aura goes through and around us. It is attached to our physical body, by a silver cord. Like the umbilical cord which detaches from our mother at birth, this silver cord detaches from our physical body when we die. This energy body continues to survive, carrying with it all its life experiences. This is how a medium can give a message from a loved one; the medium knows nothing about you or your loved one yet they are able to tell you something that you may not have told others. I do feel if a spirit gets an opportunity to communicate, they will. They want us to know that life continues, in another dimension. They know, only too well, how we long to know if there is anything once we pass away. I'm not sure why some naturally develop their sixth sense; while others can, and often do, train to develop theirs. I feel it is important for us all to learn about this other part of us, not to communicate with spirits but to benefit our lives now. We are all searching for balance. We find comfort in food, cigarettes, drugs, gambling and all kinds of things. All it does is give us a quick fix; often leaving us feeling more irritated with ourselves, but through our energy body we can find much more contentment. We go through life burying emotions we don't want to feel, many times we are left angry if someone as treated us unfairly, the key to releasing these blocked emotions is forgiveness, this can often be ourselves. If we can forgive, we are clearing blocked energy, allowing our energy to flow freely, allowing our physical body to heal itself. If we struggle to forgive someone, remember we are all born pure, many of our childhood experiences form our adult behaviour, we need to step back from a situation, try to find a reason why someone would behave the way they have.

Bible...Mathew 18. 35…

We must forgive from our heart

Bible...Mark 9.49… Everyone will be purified by fire

My interpretation….

The way I understand this, fire (hell) as many believe. If we pass away with unresolved issues, our spirit wouldn't be at peace and to burn is to destroy something. so if we can resolve through forgiveness, while still in our physical body, we have basically destroyed the negative energy; allowing us to live in peace, and rest in peace when our time comes. Life is too short for many; we never know when our time will come. So if you take no other teachings from this book, I urge you to forgive anyone (yourself maybe). You hopefully have many years ahead of you, so choose to live those in peace.

I do know that there was something unresolved with this lady who communicated with me but do not feel it is my place to write about this. Because her sons went back to their home and she no longer communicated with me, I know she is at peace.

I feel so lucky to have had such an amazing experience.

Especially now, when I am dealing with the loss of my own beautiful daughter Claire, who passed away at the young age of just twenty-five. Claire has communicated with me on at least five occasions. Without my past experience I would have either, in two of the incidents, not even acknowledged them or, the other three would have questioned my sanity.

I would say to anyone unless you are a medium, don't attempt to contact anyone who has passed away, and allow them to contact you.

1st reason) your expectation if you are doing the contacting. Our mind is capable of playing tricks on us.

2nd reason) I can't put into words how you would feel, having a loved one contact you, especially if they impress a thought on you; something you didn't know and you are able to get proof it is correct.

If anyone has had spirit activity in your home, I would advise you to contact a spiritualist church; they will advise you on how you can clear the energy in your home.

Vanessa had given me her mum's phone number. She told me that her mum would be able to teach me how to protect my aura, from other spirits who may try to communicate. So even though I was absolutely fascinated by the whole experience, it had started to take over my life. I decided to ring this lady. As soon as I walked in, she asked me to choose a ball from a box of soft different coloured balls. She asked me to throw it against the wall. I chose a dull green, she told me the colour we choose represents how we are feeling at the time. I didn't really understand what she meant but I did feel I had been left depleted of energy. I was usually buzzing with energy. She said she felt I needed to release built-up anger, I didn't feel angry, only with her telling me how she thought I was feeling. I now clearly understand, she was tuned into my energy field (aura), this was telling her what was blocking my flow of energy. If this built-up energy wasn't released, it would eventually cause me to physically express this anger towards someone. I continued throwing the ball, each time harder and harder. She was right; I knew by the way I threw the ball that I was releasing anger. She then did a guided meditation. She told me to start at the left side of my body, at my feet. Imagining that I was zipping myself into a sleeping bag. This was fine until I got to my right calf where the zip stuck. When she finished, she asked me how I felt. I said frustrated, telling her my zip had stuck. She then asked if I have any scars from past injuries. Strangely, I have two; both on my right leg, my knee and my shin. She told me that this is where my aura is weak. What I realised, years later, when I went on to practice Reiki healing, is that our aura is basically like an invisible protective shield.

A DAILY EXERCISE TO SEAL OUR AURA

Take three deep breaths, each inward breath imagine you are breathing in bright light, as you breathe out, imagine dark smoke (any built-up negative emotions). Do the exercise I was told to do. Or you can put your hands, palms facing together, above your head. Separating them as you bring them down each side of your body. Try visualising a bright light sealing itself around you or you could say the following daily affirmation.

THANK YOU. THANK YOU. THANK YOU. I AM SEALED AND PROTECTED, IN PURE LOVING ENERGY, AMEN (VISUALISING A BRIGHT LIGHT SURROUNDING YOU).

Amen ……basically means consider it done

There are many meditation CDs that can help if you struggle with the above.

(2)
My Beautiful Daughter's Tragic Short Life

August 1999

My daughter, Claire, gave birth to a beautiful baby boy. By March 2000, after many hospital appointments, Jemaine Callum was diagnosed with a rare condition, Schizencephaly and septo-optic dysplasia. This is a form of cerebral palsy. We were told that this is how it would probably affect him: he may not see, walk or talk, he would probably have seizures and challenging behaviour, his growth may also be affected due to low levels of growth hormone but if so, it could be managed with injections. We would also have to control his diet, to prevent him becoming overweight. Claire's reaction was that he was still her gorgeous little prince. Claire just lived in the moment, so didn't worry herself with what might happen. Definitely the right approach; I now practise this daily, because my thoughts almost destroyed me.

I could see a difficult life ahead of us. I only worked part-time so I offered to look after Jemaine while Claire continued her education. She studied at Wakefield Chamber of Commerce, where she won student of the year in 2000. A big achievement, considering all she had to deal with. Claire got a job in the payroll department at Sense, a charity for the deaf/blind. Claire loved her job and work colleagues; she was happy, confident and outgoing with lots of physical energy. She was eager to give her son lots of love and attention after work.

Jemaine needed regular physiotherapy because his condition causes right-side paralysis. A physiotherapist came, once a week, to do and show us exercises. I would do these during the day; Claire did them again in the evening. Claire also decided to do something that we had not been shown by his physiotherapist, so I wouldn't do these. Claire would fasten his left arm to his side, encouraging him to reach for something with his right hand. I felt this was not fair to him, I told her that she was trying to get him to do something he couldn't do. Claire said that if we didn't try, he never would. Claire had every right to feel proud when he did actually reach, even managing to grip a toy with his right hand.

My mum and dad lived on the Isle of Skye. My dad built a guest house, so they had a comfortable life. They wanted to be around to help, so they sold their home and moved back to Yorkshire. This was a big thing for them, although they never said. I know it affected them financially; and coming back to a busy city, from such a laid-back lifestyle, was not ideal.

All our family and friends were very supportive but limited in how they could help, due to Jemaine's condition. He would make very loud 'ah ah' sounds, hitting his head or head butting the floor or walls. We had to find ways of distracting him from doing this. We were told by Jemaine's paediatrician that we would have to accept that this was part of his condition; he could be provided with a helmet to protect his head.

My daughter's friend, Emma, loved coming to see him. She would take him out for walks. I'm sure this was a welcome break for Claire. When my eldest sister, Julie, and niece, Suellen, would take him out on their day off work; it was such a nice break for me. I never told Claire how much I struggled, caring for him through the day. I didn't want Claire to leave her job. I did get other breaks when my mum and dad often took Jemaine out, but I felt so guilty, they should be enjoying their grandchild, not struggling with him. How could they enjoy Jemaine when he was so unsettled?

Claire had a good social life; she had lots of friends who always visited her. She was very close to her brother, Andy, and his friends were like brothers to her. I would have Jemaine on Saturday nights, so Claire could go to clubs with her cousin, Suellen, and best friend, Andrea.

The older Jemaine got, the more I noticed how mentally delayed he was. Claire being so positive helped me to focus on what he was able to do, rather than dwelling on what he couldn't do. Claire would come home from work, so bubbly; picking Jemaine up and smothering him with kisses. Saying, "I've missed you, my little prince. I hope my little prince has been good for his grandma."

It was January 2002 when Jemaine, aged two-years-and-five-months, took his first steps. I can't find words to describe how I felt. He was very unsteady but persistent. Claire was sent an appointment to have him measured for a wheelchair his physiotherapist said even though he had started to walk due to his condition he would tire easily. Because Claire worked; I took him for the appointment. Claire asked me to tell the physiotherapist that now Jemaine had started to walk he wouldn't need one. I told the physiotherapist, who asked me to explain to Claire that he wouldn't be able to walk very far so advised us he would need a wheelchair. I told Claire that I thought it best to go with their advice. Claire said that it was not a problem if he couldn't walk far, so she refused the wheelchair. Yet another good decision. Looking back, I just wanted an easy life. I would probably have put him in the wheelchair; he would have certainly gone to school in it. Maybe he would not have continued to develop his muscles in his right leg, so there is a possible chance that he would not be walking now.

Claire must have sensed that I was struggling through the day, because she got him into a private nursery in the afternoons. I would drop him off after his dinner, Claire would pick him up when she finished work. I didn't tell her how unsettled he was when I dropped him off. She had been concerned when she picked him up, saying he always seemed very agitated. I had just been relieved to have time to myself; I knew he was in safe hands but Claire needed to know he was being stimulated, to prevent him banging his head. Jemaine would hit out at anyone or anything near him, that was in his way. He was biting his own hand, leaving teeth marks; he seemed very troubled. Claire was offered some support, from a home-based break service. Once a fortnight, a lovely young girl, Karen, would take him to the swimming baths. He loved water and was always eager to go with her. This gave Claire a nice break; she had peace of mind seeing him go off, happily.

Claire was now considering leaving her job, to care for Jemaine herself. She had tried a few nurseries, but she was always concerned that he needed more attention than the average child. Many were not equipped for Jemaine's special needs. We found out that when the children played outdoors, he was just fastened in his buggy. This would have caused him more distress seeing the children playing, especially with bikes, he would want to play with the wheels. Maybe it was more for safety, but Claire felt that he could have had a member of staff with him. We were told about Toy Box nursery, this had just opened so we thought it was worth trying, just one more. A family friend, Lindsey, worked there. She was eager to learn about Jemaine's condition and his needs. I noticed a big difference when leaving him: he was very calm. Jemaine could only say single words and they weren't very clear, but his actions spoke very clearly. Lindsey would come straight over, giving him her full attention. Claire could now continue to enjoy her job, with peace of mind. Work had many benefits; Claire had learnt to drive and bought a car. She passed level one in sign language, eager to continue, hoping for a career in sign language. Jemaine loved being driven about, it made life so much easier. She could now take him with her when she went shopping. One day, Claire called to see me after they had been out shopping. She was very upset; Jemaine had hit a woman as she was passing him, and the woman was very angry. She walked away, without giving Claire a chance to explain about his condition. Claire felt the woman just saw him as a naughty child, whose mother could not control him. This was the start of Claire having panic attacks. She had enjoyed their shopping trips up until then. Her little son who we thought wouldn't walk, would push the big trolley around. She didn't mind the fight to stop the trolley bumping into things, she was just so proud of the things he could do. Jemaine was now old enough to leave Toy Box private nursery and start St. Michael's nursery. There were lots of staff so keeping him entertained wasn't a problem. Also, he loved being outdoors. He had an obsession with wheels and there were plenty of bikes, so we knew he would be happy there. When he was old enough, he got a statement giving him a place in mainstream school, with a one-to-one teaching assistant. This was not only good for Jemaine, but also for the other children, who would learn, from a young age, to accept children with special needs. They were very kind to him in school, but outside school he just saw family and Claire's friend's daughter. He got an invitation to Jack's party, a boy in his class, Claire was so happy because the only parties he was invited to were a friend Jacob who had special needs. When Claire and I would play in the garden with Jemaine, Claire would say I just wish Jemaine could play with the other children. Claire had read a story about a lady, who paid a young boy to play with her special needs son. This really upset her to think her son could grow up without friends. Jemaine's teaching assistant was a lovely lady, Sue. She must have had so much patience; she worked hard, helping him develop. She also tried to prevent him hitting out or banging his head and biting his hand. There weren't the toys he had played with in nursery; he now had to participate in class routine. So I admire Sue and any of these teaching assistants, they make a difficult job look easy. Claire would pick Jemaine up from my house when she finished work. She had always walked in the house, very excited and eager to see her little prince; but I noticed she wasn't her bubbly self. She wasn't seeing many of her friends anymore. I thought maybe now that she's driving, it could be she wasn't home as much.

Jemaine was getting more difficult to care for, the older he got. I would go round each morning, to help get him ready for school, because of his right-side paralysis he wore a splint on his right leg, this was to help correct the position of his foot, without this he would walk on his toes, it took both of us to get this on him as he didn't like wearing it. It was upsetting for me, so I could imagine this wouldn't be a good start to Claire's day. Jemaine, now age seven, was given three overnight stays a month at Wasdale Respite Care home. This was to benefit Claire and myself to give us some free time to focus on something other than caring for Jemaine. The staff were really friendly so Jemaine settled in well. They went out to parks and did lots of activities. Claire was happy for him to go, so I knew she needed the break. It was the start of the school holidays; I was waiting in the playground when a young girl came over to me asking if she could have Jemaine one day during the school holidays. I felt my prayers had been answered; it was as if an angel had come to my aid. Having Jemaine at home all day, when I was used to just having him from three p.m. until five p.m. was tiring; just thinking how I would occupy him. I thought, how lovely. Emma, who had a son of her own, wanted to give her own time to have Jemaine. This made Claire really happy; someone other than family, and the few close friends, wanted her son. Emma worked in school, so we knew he would be well looked after. Emma started taking him regularly; he was treated like a member of her family. She took him on outings, he was always happy to go with her.

Jemaine was now struggling to fit in with class routine, so we moved him to Kingsland special needs school. I was hiding my true feelings. I felt sad that he could no longer go to mainstream school, which was a selfish thought because Kingsland School had so much more to offer. They had a sensory room, equipment essential for calming him and helping in his development. Also, all staff are well trained to cope with his condition.

Claire had been practising yoga and meditation, also having Reiki on the nights Jemaine was at Wasdale. These things had helped Claire with the anxiety, which kept creeping back in whenever she had something she was struggling with. Claire had always been a naturally positive girl but because the panic attacks came back, I suggested she leave her job, giving her time for herself during the day. Claire did leave, but didn't feel being at home was for her, so she got various qualifications in beauty therapy and opened up a shop. Sadly, the panic attacks came back so she closed her shop.

One day, I called during the day to see Claire. I could not see her room floor, for piles of papers. I could now understand why she closed her shop. How could I have not seen how much she had to deal with, on top of her now very demanding son? There were piles of letters from tax credits, demanding repayment for overpayment, apparently they did not receive Claire's annual declaration in time, so this is classed as an overpayment. She had made endless calls, trying to resolve this. Even though Claire was financially comfortable she felt she had been treated unfairly so needed to resolve this. There was also a pile of gas bills, she didn't even have gas connected to her home. A fine for displaying Jemaine's badge upside down, she had queried this but then paid it. Yet, the demands were still coming. The list was endless; Claire had been trying to deal with these things for quite a while. I tried to sort some myself, but Claire being an adult had to give consent. By the time she got to speak with someone, it was easier to try and resolve it herself.

Claire's friend, Shaz, asked if they wanted a holiday to Dominican Republic. It was just what she needed; also she could have her dream of Jemaine swimming with dolphins. She was very excited, I saw my old daughter back at last. Shopping for their holiday clothes, she had always loved shopping. Shaz was so good with Jemaine, so off they went for two weeks. The holiday did her the world of good. Yes, the mountain of paperwork was still there; but it's easier to deal with when you have a positive attitude.

Claire's brother, Andy, was now in a relationship with a lovely girl, Sally. Her eldest son, Jordon, was adorable. He would go spend time, just sitting with Jemaine; he had such a calming effect on Jemaine. Jemaine copied other children's behaviour, so he also copied Jordon by just sitting calmly; something he rarely did. Claire and Jemaine went on family outings with Andy, Sally and her children, which they really enjoyed. Other than his cousins – Chloe, Mikey and baby Anisa – he didn't spend time round other children, out of school or Wasdale.

2009, THE YEAR OF HELL! Jemaine had now started having seizures. This was such a worry for Claire, she said, "As if my son hasn't enough to deal with."

He was given medication, but it didn't stop the seizures. Claire didn't want him to go to Wasdale anymore, she thought he could have a seizure through the night and die. I tried to reassure her that the staff were well trained and would take extra care. He continued to go but this was no longer the welcome break for Claire it had been, but constant worry. Even when he slept at my house, she would ring to check how he was. I would tell her to enjoy her free time. All the worry brought on the panic attacks again. The mountain of paperwork didn't go down; if anything did get resolved, there was something else to replace it. Claire's sleep was troubled with nightmares, so each morning she would wake exhausted. Claire would tell me her dreams (nightmares); she was either being chased or surrounded by big spiders. One night, when Jemaine was at Wasdale, I slept at Claire's. She was dreaming, making sounds like she was scared. I woke her, asking if she was okay, she just said, "Yes, why?"

She fell straight back to sleep. I could now understand why she was so exhausted.

Jemaine came home from school one day, his face was bright red and puffy and he was screaming out in pain. This was far worse than he had been before. I rang the doctor, who came quite quickly, but he must have thought I was overreacting. Because Jemaine was so calm when the doctor arrived. The doctor checked him but found nothing wrong, not even a high temperature.

It was now the start of the six-week summer holidays. Jemaine was totally out of control, hitting out at anyone, biting his own hand, head butting, making repetitive ah sounds. He seemed in so much pain, but we just had to accept that this was part of his condition. We had been told that his condition would probably get worse, as he got older. He would need a helmet to protect his head but I never thought anything like this, this was a living hell for the three of us. Claire seemed to be a magnet for anything negative; she was only leaving her house to do her shopping.

I took Claire to the doctor, hoping to get some counselling. Claire was diagnosed with bi-polar, given medication and counselled at home. This was not an ideal situation, with Jemaine pacing the room saying, “Ah, ah, ah,” constantly. Neither Claire nor I could cope on our own with Jemaine, he had so much energy; we were physically and mentally drained caring for him.

Claire had always been in good physical health, she rang me saying her legs were numb and feet were freezing. I went round to her house and massaged her legs, but could not warm them. Her body was hot, but below her knees, her legs were so cold. Claire’s medication had been changed, but the only difference, that I noticed, was that she seemed distant. Claire would give everyone a big hug when she saw them but now seemed cold towards us. One day, while Claire was staying with me, she got really ill. I called for an ambulance, she was holding her head in agony and she couldn’t feel her legs. She was carried into the ambulance. I had Jemaine, so couldn’t go with her. She came home a few hours later, perfectly well, with no treatment or explanation about why she had gotten so ill. This happened again. She was treated for swine flu when she hadn’t left her house or been in contact with anyone who had it. One day, she was at my house and I actually took a photo to show the doctor because she looked so ill. I walked her round home, where she collapsed on her kitchen floor, crying in pain and holding her head. I videoed this also; because if she just got well again, at least I could show her doctor how bright red her face was and the pain she was in. Her medication was changed. It was Jemaine’s turn again. He was rushed to hospital with suspected swine flu. By the time they got him to casualty, he was perfectly well; he was sent home after being examined without any treatment, which confirmed to me that Claire’s wasn’t swine flu either. What on earth was going on? I got up at six a.m. each morning, to start my day with a prayer. I believe this saved me from having a breakdown. Everything seemed out of our control. My mum and dad would still take Jemaine, to give us a break. I don't know how they coped; they must have really struggled. Claire had kept her paperwork to herself, so as not to burden me. I was not telling mum and dad how ill Claire and Jemaine kept being, so as not to cause them any more worry. I think they were not telling us that Jemaine was too much for them to cope with because they knew we needed a break. It seems we were all trying to protect each other.

It was now Christmas; Claire was usually so excited, like a giddy little child. Although her car was filled with gifts for everyone as always, she wasn't her bubbly self. Numb is the only way to describe her.

UNCONDITIONAL LOVE

One day, during the school summer holidays 2009, I had gone to see Claire and Jemaine; it was one of many chaotic days, there was a knock at Claire's door. I opened the door to a young girl and boy, about eleven or twelve-years-old. The girl asked if Claire was in. I felt that everyone who went to Claire's wanted something from her. I walked into the room saying, "There are two parasites at your door."

Claire anxiously put her finger to her mouth saying, "Sshh," and indicating they would hear me. Claire went to the door, I heard the girl ask if they could have a drink, please. Claire went to her fridge, got two cans of pop and two packets of crisps. I was fuming, as I asked Claire, "Where are their parents? They're probably in the pub, they don't care if their kids are thirsty, so why should you?"

Claire said, "I don't know where their parents are but it doesn't mean I don't have to care." This is a memory that will stay clear in my mind. If I could go back to that day, I would tell Claire how proud I was of her being such a caring person. How we treat children when they are growing up can have a big influence on how they treat people. But Claire would not have been trying to teach them anything, simply just caring. At the time, I was practising Reiki and teaching others that we should all treat each other with love and respect. What a hypocrite and I didn't even realise it. I am no hypocrite now, I will continue to love and care; give and share, the way my daughter naturally did. I also look back, remembering at the time, I was making donations to what I felt to be a good cause. I thought people took advantage of Claire's kind nature, not seeing it was Claire's choice to give.

Bible…Mathew…6.5.
Don't expect anything in return when helping others
Bible…Acts…20.25.
More happiness in giving than receiving
Bible…Mark…10.21.
Give to those in need, you will receive riches in heaven

RECEIVING SIGHT / RECEIVE INSIGHT

Physical sight / spiritual sight

When you say receiving sight and receive insight, it sounds the same, but relates to our physical sight we are usually born with, but also our spiritual sight, (insight) this is our intuition that can guide us once we understand we have this ability. Our childhood forms who we become as an adult, we then make our own choices. Many of us will take any job because we need to support ourselves, we often complain we don't get satisfaction from our work. We will all have days when we don't feel like going to work, but if you really don't enjoy your job then practise meditation, it will allow your intuition to guide you. You will see an opportunity and a knowing, (a kind of warm almost like goose bumps feeling) this is something you would get a lot of satisfaction from. Try not to worry about money because believe me, if it's what you're meant to be doing, it will all fall into place. I had no ambitions; I've plodded through life, luckily working with some lovely people. However, not until Claire had Jemaine did I realise what my purpose was. Looking back, I can see how I have taken an alternative route to counselling. Thankfully, Claire having Jemaine opened my eyes to a whole new understanding of life. My experiences, as tragic as they are, have allowed me to help others make changes to better their lives, I am eternally grateful to my daughter for leading me on this path.

(3)
A Journey through Hell

When my grandson was born, I knew my life would change but not to the extent it has. When Jemaine was three-months-old, I sat having a cuppa with my friend, Janine, and Jemaine was sitting between my legs on the floor. I looked down and noticed his head seemed flat at one side; I burst out crying and told Janine there was something wrong with him. I knew he had come to no harm; he was always in safe hands. I'd often heard people talk about their gut feeling, but even at forty-years-old, I thought it was just a saying. I had a feeling deep inside me, knowing something was wrong with him. The next day Audra took me to the doctor's with him, without saying anything to Claire. The doctor tried to reassure me babies often have unusually shaped heads, saying pressure during delivery can cause this. He said it was nothing of concern, but did arrange for some tests. When our babies are born we seem to inspect every little part of them, I would have noticed the shape of his head. Over the next few months Claire took him for quite a few appointments. I told her these were routine tests, I didn't want to worry her and I hoped I was wrong with this gut feeling. Even though I had felt something was wrong, I had not prepared myself for what Claire told me. I had never heard of Schizencephaly but it sounded like a serious condition. My first thoughts when Claire told me about his condition were, *How can a child with so many problems have a purpose in life?*

I hate to admit this but felt he was a burden. I now know that he is a very special child who has taught me unconditional love. I was managing to stay reasonably strong in front of Claire, but I was crying myself to sleep. I just wanted to wake and have it been a bad dream. By the time Jemaine was twelve-months-old, I had to go to the doctor's because I was not able to control my emotions through the day and I was a wreck. The doctor gave me anti-depressants. After three days of taking these, I was in town and I saw a sign in a shop window saying 'Reiki'. My gut feeling was talking to me again. When Jemaine was about two-months-old, a clairvoyant had given me a psychic reading, she said I had a gift of healing and went on to tell me how I could go about developing this. I was not interested in this Reiki healing that she was telling me I could be doing. I felt irritated, I had not heard of it and I did not want to. Now I was drawn to this word, Reiki, I wanted to know more, I felt maybe this could take away my pain. I went in the shop and was told that it is an attunement you have. I knew I had to have this, whatever it was. The next day I paid £100, it was money well spent. I did not understand what I had done, all I know is I felt I could take on the world. I threw away the anti-depressants and approached life with a different attitude. I must have been a real pain to my family and friends. I had been shown a scanning technique, where you put your hand above a person, you have no physical contact, yet you are able to tell them something about their health you couldn't possibly know.

This gave me a big ego, which can be very destructive, so luckily I got busy taking Jemaine for appointments. Although I wasn't practising Reiki, I managed to stay reasonably positive. Claire was so bubbly, always so happy when she came to pick Jemaine up after work, so no matter how I had been feeling, Claire would instantly make me feel better.

One day, a leaflet came through the door. I would normally throw anything that wasn't post in the bin, they were courses on Reiki and psychic awareness. *Here we go again*, my gut feeling was telling me to enrol in this course especially when I saw who was taking the class. Leanne Davis, the lady who did my reading, she was not a teacher at the time of my reading. She had not influenced me in any way, everything I was doing was using my intuition. I was given a recording of my reading, when I play it back she had told me things about my future that she couldn't have known. She had never met me before doing my reading. I went on the course and learnt so much about our aura, how we affect, infect in some cases, people we come into contact with. We don't even have to speak. I met a lovely lady on this course, Jo. She taught me so much about Reiki and crystals, I had my second attunement with her. The buzz came back, but this time I wanted to take it slowly. Reiki is so much more than healing our physical body; it becomes a way of life that benefits all areas.

Over the next few years, Claire and I used Reiki and meditation, to help calm our minds. Life was always testing us; just when we felt we were getting on top of things, something else would be thrown at us. It was now 2009, I was having amazing experiences with Reiki, but home life was so hectic. I no longer did Reiki on Claire, and looking back, I can't really understand why I didn't make time because we both benefitted from it so much. One day, I had an amazing experience during a meditation. I was lying on my bed, in my Reiki room, but in my mind, I was in a meadow. The meadow was filled with dandelions, the seeds were flying about tickling my face and it felt so real. I opened my eyes expecting to be in a meadow, to think here I am laying on my bed, yet in my mind, I am somewhere else. I'd been telling people about the benefits of meditation, so I told them about this, telling Claire we really need to meditate more. I know our peace lies in meditation.

DECEMBER 29th, 2009. The worst day of my life, I went to Claire's house to find her lying on her bed, still in her nightwear, although she was breathing I couldn't get any response. I called 999, but my gut feeling was talking to me yet again. I had a knowing deep inside, my beautiful daughter's life was ending. Claire was taken to the intensive care unit, which gave me hope my gut feeling would hopefully be wrong this time.

DECEMBER 30th. The life support machine was turned off, my gut feeling had been right. Claire's dad, brother and I left the hospital numb. They say you go into shock when you lose a close loved one, I can understand this. You feel so empty and you have no idea what to say to each other. How I managed to tell my parents, who absolutely loved their granddaughter, I don't know. I can see and hear clearly, to this day, their reaction. When night time came, I felt the pain so intensely, it really hit me. I would never again feel my daughter hug me or hear her excited voice telling me something Jemaine had done. But in my mind, her voice was real saying, *Clever boy, Jemaine.* It was something she said almost every day. Give me a toothache, childbirth, anything but this. I thought night time was unbearable but when morning came, all I wanted was night time to come again so I didn't have to face anyone. How could I face the day? My sister, Mandy, and my mum and dad came to take Jemaine and myself out for lunch on New Year's Day. I can't imagine why we would want to eat out within two days of Claire passing, all I can think is that we were trying to take our minds off the reality of what we were facing. We were driving round trying to find a place to eat, Jemaine just burst out laughing. He couldn't stop, he was hysterical. It was such a contagious laugh that we couldn't help but laugh ourselves, even though we had no idea what he was laughing at. Because of my past experience with spirits, I felt that Claire was probably making him laugh to change the energy. We all just sat in the car, not knowing what to say. Even my family began to wonder if there could be something happening to do with Claire because this was something Jemaine had never done before. Yes the occasional giggle, but not this continued belly laughter for a good ten minutes, a long time to laugh at nothing. Over the next few days we had so many visitors and phone calls, even school friends who didn't really know what to say but wanted to let us know they were thinking of us. One minute we were all crying, then laughing at funny things Claire had said and done. We had to carry on the best we could for Jemaine. It was snowing so we played out, snowballing and making a snowman. I can't imagine what my neighbours would have thought as we snowballed each other, playing as if nothing had happened. My son, Andy, and nephew, Kev, came and took Jemaine sledging. In fact, when the rest of our family heard, they all went along. I just wanted time to myself so I stayed home. We were just trying to do the best we could to get through the day.

2nd January, I went to do some washing. I pressed the on button, it didn't light up and there was nothing happening. So my husband, Trev, pulled the washer out from under the worktop. I reached to the back of the units, unplugged the washer, passed the plug to Trev to put a new fuse in. He put one in, then I plugged it back in and pressed the switch on by the plug. I then realised I had not turned the switch off. We pressed the washer switch, it worked, so I asked Trev to put the old fuse back in. He did and I plugged it in and the washer worked, it had been turned off at the switch by the plug, no one could have done this. I knew my daughter was no longer in her physical body, but around us in spirit, getting our attention.

Eight days after Claire passed away, she came to me in a dream, repeating the words 'miss adventure'. Because we didn't know what had happened to her, I knew she was trying to tell me something, but didn't understand what. I thought miss because she wasn't married and something about an adventure. I told Trev the next morning, he said it's a term they use at an inquest, my mum and dad said it means cause unknown. Even though I was told an autopsy would be carried out to find the cause of Claire's death, I did not know of any terms they use , nor would I want this to be the verdict, any mother would want to know the cause of her child's death. I told my family and friends, this would be the verdict. I knew Claire wanted us to know life does go on. Because I have no knowledge of inquests this would be proof.

Claire, absolutely adored Jordon (Katie Price). Harvey and Jemaine's, conditions are very similar, she would have loved to have met Katie. So for Claire's funeral I chose the horses and carriage; because my daughter would never have the wedding, she dreamed of, like Katie and Peter. The day of the funeral must have been one of the coldest days on record, yet so many friends and family turned out to pay their respects. Wasdale staff were so helpful, they took Jemaine to the church, to take any pressure off us. I was so proud of him, there were no repetitive sounds or banging his head, he was so calm. Everyone commented on how well behaved he was. 30th JUNE. Sure enough the verdict MISADVENTURE.

Misadventure (cause unknown) I have to accept this. Even though I know, through documentaries, that they can tell you the cause of death of someone who's been found years after they have died. I believe there is a heaven, Claire has been taken into heaven from what had become hell.

Bible……John.20.17.

Don't hold on to loved ones who have passed, allow them to go to heaven.

(4)
Our Broken Hearts

Jemaine, now aged ten, seemed to cope quite well at first. He would go to our door and say, "Mummy", for me to take him to his mummy's house. It was so difficult for me to take him. Their house was still the same as when they had lived there, a cosy clean home, but now had a cold depressing feel to it. He would walk round each room, his hand in the calling position, calling his mummy. Because he is mentally delayed I didn't feel he understood heaven, so I said, "Mummy's gone."

We have to use as few words as possible for him to understand. I would collapse into a chair and sob, he would just carry on calling mummy. I would get myself together and hope I wouldn't see anyone on my way back home because I looked shocking with all the crying. It was Mother's Day when I realised, why he had accepted mummy wasn't home. He came home from school with a card he had made, I asked him for it but he said firmly, "NO! MUMMY."

I once again took him to his house, so he could see she wasn't there. He did the usual thing calling mummy, I did the usual sobbing thing, but I also videoed him. It was the kind of moment you want to catch to show someone, but how could I show my family something so upsetting. He came away okay but still wouldn't give me the card, he even put it under his pillow at bedtime. The next day I asked Trev to take us to the cemetery, hopefully he would then understand. We got to the top of the road to turn left, he wanted to turn right, so Trev followed his directions. He took us to the A&E department at Pinderfields hospital. I then realised he had been taken to A&E just weeks before he had seen his mummy taken away in the ambulance. All this time he had thought his mummy was in hospital, each time I had taken him home he had expected his mummy be home from hospital. I just fell apart, I didn't feel I could cope much more. We did eventually get to the cemetery, he reluctantly left his card, but I didn't feel he understood.

I struggled so much each morning getting Jemaine ready for school, he would kick and head-butt me. I would be crying as I was dressing him, thinking how much more can I take, he would then be picked up for school. There's something soothing about a cup of tea or coffee, although only temporary it gives you a break to regain some sanity. Shaz, Claire's friend who took them on holiday, would come regularly to take Jemaine to give me a break. I so appreciated it, they had quite a strong bond. Shaz was also a carer so I knew she would be okay if Jemaine had a seizure. Wasdale were so good with extra overnights offered to me if they had a cancellation. Two lovely girls, Tracy and Nicky, from Home-based Break Scheme came once a week to take Jemaine out for a few hours. He was still very hard to control, so they must have struggled to keep him entertained. My mum and dad would come to take Jemaine out, I wanted the break, but my parents were seventy at the time. I could barely cope with him, so I know they would have struggled. It was also heartbreaking each time I saw my parents, we were all trying so hard to be strong but I always wanted to talk about Claire, even though I knew we would all end up in tears. They brought him home one day, my mum said he had run off, we then started to go places together. It was still a break away from home. Lindsey, from Toy Box nursery, got in touch asking if she could start taking him out. One day, when Lindsey arranged to come for him, it was thick with snow yet she still turned up for him. I got many phone calls, even friends from school, asking how I was coping. Usually, I would have a cry then get my strength back and reassure my friends I was okay, only to put down the phone and sob like a baby. No one can take this pain away, but it is nice to know everyone cares.

The beginning of August 2010, I got a call from my sister, Mandy, telling me that she and my niece were coming to visit. I was looking forward to seeing them, not aware there was more upset for us. Rachel, aged twenty-five, had just been diagnosed with stage four cervical cancer. I reacted so calmly because I was getting used to my gut feeling by now and thankfully it was telling me she's going to be fine. It was upsetting seeing Rachel when she started losing her hair, but she got some lovely hairpieces which really suited her. Rachel never lost her sense of humour, with her positive attitude you almost forgot she was ill. If she hadn't told us, we probably wouldn't have guessed. Thankfully Rachel is now very healthy, living her life to the fullest.

EPHESIAN.	6.12.	FIGHTING DARK FORCES, DARK AGE
HOSEA.	5.15.	IN OUR SUFFERING WE WILL FIND OUR TRUE SELF
PETER.	4.12.	PAINFUL TEST YOU ARE SUFFERING, ALL PART OF GODS PLAN
2 TIMOTHY 3		DIFFICULT TIMES IN THE LAST DAYS

August 2010 we had a family holiday, a camping holiday in Scarborough. Partway through the holiday we had gone to the amusement arcades. I somehow ended up at the top overlooking the sea, above all the arcades near some memorial. Claire and I had been to Scarborough for her birthday the year before. I was now in the same spot where Claire had stood at four a.m. with her arms outstretched in a lovely coral dress, looking so content and beautiful. I went from sadness to anger, how could I enjoy a holiday with my family when my daughter cannot be here to enjoy her life? I managed to hide my feelings from my family but when I got home from holiday I sent a text message to my sisters telling them not to contact me, telling them they had done nothing wrong but I needed time to myself. I was an absolute wreck. Jemaine had been so well behaved yet I felt so angry, I wanted my daughter. I remember my friend, Jill, who lost her daughter, Olivia, many years ago. She told me I would go through feelings of anger, bitterness, guilt, resentment, etc. At the time I thought, *No I wouldn't,* because I had been teaching others through Reiki how destructive these emotions are. Here

I was now, feeling anger and resentment towards everyone, even my own family who were also missing Claire. I needed more time for myself to deal with these feelings. I contacted, Carol-Ann our social worker, she got Jemaine a place at York Villas respite care home two nights a week. He had been so settled at Wasdale I didn't want any more upset for him, but now I really had to think about my own health. Wasdale had only been able to offer three nights each month. The staff at York Villas were just as caring as Wasdale staff so he adapted to the change quite well. Since Jemaine came into our lives, I have met some of the nicest people. Yes, it is a job they do, but a very demanding one. It takes a special person to work with a special needs child.

WE DON'T HAVE TO DIE, TO REST IN PEACE, WE NEED TO WAKE UP, TO WHAT LIFE IS TRULY ABOUT IF WE SLOW DOWN LIVE IN THE MOMENT ENJOY OUR JOURNEY. WE CAN THEN REST IN PEACE EACH NIGHT

****

WHEN WE FOCUS ON SOMEONE ELSE, GOING OUT OF OUR WAY TO MAKE THEIR LIFE BETTER, WE HAVE RECEIVED OUR OWN HEALING. STAYING FOCUSED IS THE KEY, WHAT WE GIVE OUT WE WILL RECEIVE.

GIVE LOVE, RECEIVE LOVE

(5)
Jemaine's Relief from Seizures / My Physical suffering

2011. Trev recorded a true movie, about a boy with epilepsy. His seizures were controlled by a diet (ketogenic diet). I asked Jemaine's paediatrician if he could go on this diet, he told me there was a long waiting list. He had been on various medications, from 2009, these had no effect and he was having seizures all the time. I started to prepare him for this diet, by cutting down his sugary foods, I couldn't believe what happened. His seizures stopped and his behaviour calmed. He was a different child. Even the head-butting the floor and the repetitive ah sounds stopped. I had previously given him biscuits, chocolate and lots of juice to keep him quiet. While he was eating, he wasn't making the repetitive sounds. I never did get him on the diet, he no longer needed it.

Once he was seizure-free for a year, this was 22 August 2012, the doctor allowed him to stop the medication; telling me there was a strong possibility the seizures would start again. They didn't; he has had an occasional seizure, in the last five years. Strangely, while I have been writing this story, he has had about three in a few weeks. He does carry a rescue remedy. I would not recommend anyone make any changes to any medication. I had previously told Claire to stop giving him the medication, he had taken it about three months with no change so I didn't see the point in giving it to him. I didn't realise you have to be weaned off it; any immediate change can actually bring on seizures. This had happened earlier in 2009, when he had to be admitted to hospital due to a few seizures in one day. Because of this past experience, although the seizures stopped, I was now fully aware we must always follow any medical advice. I continued to give him medication until his paediatrician allowed him to stop taking it.

Life was getting easier, with the weekly respite care. Claire's best friend, Andrea, and Aji, a care worker who had worked with Jemaine at Wasdale, got in touch to see if they could start taking Jemaine out. How lovely, they both work full time, yet they want to give their free time to spend with Jemaine. Since 2006, I had been getting up at 05:55 a.m. to start my day with a prayer. In 2011, I was now asking in prayer for my skin to be youthful and vibrant. I felt I had aged so much with all the crying. Not long after, I started waking up throughout the night with itchy skin, it was making my life a misery. I couldn't help myself, no matter how much Reiki/meditation I did. I used steroid creams and anti-histamines. I had started eating healthier in 2009, but this didn't make any difference. Three of my friends – Sharon, Donna and Susan – did free treatments of hypnosis, Reiki and reflexology. I did get some relief from these, but deep down I knew Susan was right when she told me where she thought the root of my problem was. I needed to forgive the people who were irritating me, it was no one's fault Claire wasn't here. It's not easy to forgive, I was struggling because my mind kept reminding me what someone had said or done. I tried to visualise a stop sign, saying to myself, "This person would never intentionally want to upset me."

I now realise that I must have been so annoying when anyone had Reiki. I would tell them to SIMPLY forgive whoever they had an issue with and their body could then heal. I will be more understanding now; it is not an easy thing to do but it is necessary.

(6)
Update 20

It's been almost eight years since Claire passed away. Starting my day with a daily prayer, for me, is not about religion. It's a way to connect every part of me; my mind, body and spirit. Allowing me to feel close to Claire, I'd love nothing more than to cuddle Claire but that is not possible. So this is the next best thing. I thank Claire for the twenty-five years I was blessed with her. I still have days where I cry uncontrollably. One of those days was 2016, again it was Mother's Day, all our family met at the cemetery. Claire's Castle, as my nephew Mikey calls it. Jemaine had, previously, always been irritable, hitting the headstone, being quite angry. This day he was different, he started saying, "Mummy, get up please." He kept pleading, repeating, "Mummy, get up."

I managed to tell him his mummy couldn't get up and he calmly walked away. I got him into the car and we left. I couldn't even say bye to anyone, I needed to get him home so I could allow myself to cry without upsetting my family. I did feel that, at last, he understands this is where his mummy is; he has been okay when visiting since but doesn't like to stay for too long.

When I video Jemaine, there are always white particles floating around him. Trev has the same phone as me but does not get these particles on his videos. Some say it is dust.

Bible.

Ecclesiastes...3.20.

We come from dust, we return to dust.

This Christmas, when I videoed Jemaine not only was there particles, but there was also a spark of light, like a sparkler. There is no explanation for this. I know it is Claire's energy because of my past experience with spirits.

Jemaine is a handsome, healthy, happy and polite young man. Being partially sighted does not seem to restrict him from doing anything. He doesn't like long walks but will join in if a group are out walking. He has specially designed boots, these have helped correct the position of his right foot. He never needed growth hormone injections, he is quite tall for his age. He cannot say a full sentence, but can say enough to make his needs known. He is mentally delayed but manages to use his iPad with ease. Even going on Google Earth, to show me a Chinese takeaway, to show me what he wants for tea. He keeps constant watch of the time; he set my alarm on my phone for six thirty a.m. to get up for school, and 06:40 on Saturdays for a ten-minute lay in. Despite right-side paralysis, he learnt to swim, at thirteen, doing the doggy paddle. He has an obsession with washing machines, even telling people what cycle their clothes need to be washed on. I know Claire will be so proud of him. Other than Jordon, Jemaine has not really had a friend to go for days out. I would dread the school summer holidays, even though he went to York Villas. The days seemed so long, my parents couldn't take him to give me a break; although he wasn't having seizures, he had to be with someone who is trained in giving buccolam (rescue remedy), in case of prolonged seizures. So when staff at York Villas told me Jacob and Jemaine had become friends, I knew it was yet another prayer answered. Jacob's mum, Fiona, has a heart of gold; we have known each other from a physiotherapy group when the boys were very young. After Claire passed away, Fiona was very supportive and often sent random gifts and cards in the post. I am not materialistic, but to know someone is thinking of you and your unbearable situation, when her own life was very demanding, meant so much. I had often wished the boys would be friends, so we could have days out. (I always say thank you, thank you, thank you, when I know a prayer is answered.)

It is August 2017, the past month has been nothing but heartache for me. Jemaine turned eighteen on the 24th of August, so he left York Villas and home. He has moved in with a lovely couple, Holly and Tom; this was intended as shared living, with Jemaine coming home each weekend. I decided it was best for him to go, permanently, as I could not handle the upset of taking him back after the weekend. Jemaine was so grown up about it. He, happily, left York Villas saying, "[he] is big now, [he's] 18."

He's so comical. Hugging the female staff saying, "Bye, sweetheart," high-fiving all the male staff. He came home with lots of gifts, including a suitcase which he started to pack when we got home from his last overnight stay on the 23rd. We took him to Holly's, at teatime, on his birthday. It was heart-breaking, leaving him, even though he is very happy. It left me feeling so deflated. I felt lost, even though I can take him out whenever I want. I have to accept that change is often for our own good.

I open my Bible randomly each morning. I have done this for many years, so now I clearly understand the messages. Jesus talks in parables, which I believe is for us to work out what the messages are telling us. Therefore stimulating our minds, I see it as a daily mind workout. Why else would it be written that way?

I also have a book which belonged to Claire, *God Calling*, it has a message for each day of the year. Giving us strength to face our troubles, with the clear message throughout the book. It's in our troubles we find our inner strength. Some may think this book did not help my daughter, but yes it did. Claire had pencilled a line, under certain teachings that were relevant to her life. If I do this, it is because I will pass the book on; wanting the next reader to take particular note of what is written.

Since Claire passed away, I have noticed lots of young people around Claire's age have also passed. Many of these, it seems, are things we can learn to prevent. Car accident, was someone going too fast? Losing control with NO intention of loss of life? Taking drugs, many just want to fit in so they do what seems to be the cool thing. Alcohol, many drink too much to give them confidence or forget any troubles. Suicide, no one who bullies someone would want that person to end their life. Usually someone who bullies another is insecure so they find a weaker person than themselves, but would not do this if they truly understood the misery they were causing them. Someone may take their own life, with a belief that others are better off without them. This is never so. We are often too wrapped up in our own lives to recognise someone is struggling, needing encouragement to get them through a temporary situation.

Bible

Romans…… 13.8

Whether we live or die, all part of God's plan

Peter..………5.9

suffering doing God's will

2 Timothy…1.8.

Don't be ashamed to talk about God, take your part in suffering.

(7)
Aura

Here is a photograph I had taken in 2002, using Kirlian photography.

Dr Kirlian discovered he was able to photograph our aura in 1959. The layers of colour represent things about our health. You will notice pictures of Jesus with a blue/white Aura

Bible……1 CORINTHIANS13.12
What we see now is like a dim image in a mirror

Bible ….1 CORINTHIANS 13.12
Then we shall see face to face.
(As we are now able to see with Aura photography,
as in my aura photograph)

Our soul is the intelligence within us, which connects us as one. Our aura can only be seen by someone who has auric vision. In 1959, Dr Kirlian discovered the aura can be photographed with special equipment. Named after himself, Kirlian photography. They took a photo of a healthy plant, there was a gap in its aura; within a short time the leaf, where the gap was, fell off. The gap in the aura was obviously showing something, was happening in the plant, before the leaf died. Our energy body goes through and around our physical body. It has seven main energy centres, called chakras. Each chakra relates to a different part of the body. As we feed our physical body food, we should also feed our energy body (aura). One way we feed it is to acknowledge we have this. With palms facing each other, rub your hands together really fast. With palms still facing, slowly separate them about six inches apart then push them slowly towards each other almost touching. Separate them again; you may feel tingling, heat, cold, or pulsing. If you put your hand above your head, about four inches away, you may feel your head tingle. Pets are sensitive to our energy, so you could hold your hand just above your pet after rubbing your hands fast; a cat will purr and settle, for you to continue sending energy towards it. Even if you don't experience anything, keep practicing when you have free time. Ways to feed our aura are meditation, having holistic treatments, even reading spiritual books. If you're someone who eats when you're not hungry, next time instead of eating, try just sitting in silence. You will probably feel irritable but if you resist the urge to get some food, you may notice a random thought about your past. This is your aura taking the opportunity to cleanse itself, of a past negative energy pattern. You are feeding your aura, instead of your physical, therefore your aura expands. Instead of overeating and your physical body getting bigger. Not that size matters, it's about how content we are in ourselves.

Claire had a lovely, clean, comfortable and cosy home, but once negative energy builds up, it doesn't matter how clean our home is, it's our aura we need to clean. Our surroundings reflect what's going on in our own energy. All the amount of paperwork, forms to be filled in and documents needed for proof; these need to be photo-copied. Computers and photocopiers are often unreliable, this results in more stress. Which is a vicious circle, of more of what we are focusing on. So even if something was completed, there would be something else to replace it. When I first became aware of the amount of paperwork, I angrily asked how it had built up to all this. I was unconsciously fuelling this negative energy because my attitude was negative. Even when I tried helping Claire, the energy I was feeling was frustration, so would not help. One thing I would change, to take stress of a parent of a special needs child, is when a child is diagnosed with a disability/life-affecting condition, the hospital number they are given should be sufficient for any benefit claim. So when they need to apply for anything, they could simply give their number. Which can then access all their information, about their condition, which would be accurate due to regular appointments; showing any improvement or deterioration of their condition. Life caring, for a special needs child, is stressful enough without all these time-consuming forms. I have had these forms to complete, when Jemaine lived with me, and have felt mentally drained after completing just one form to claim DLA. So to think how Claire must have felt, with so many other things to deal with. Well, I just can't allow myself to stay with that thought, it is much too painful.

(8)
Reiki

Reiki is working on our Aura, (energy body). Often, when we experience something embarrassing or humiliating or losing a loved one. We don't want to feel the pain, we try to avoid dealing with it and we push it deep inside; trying to forget it happened. At some point, later in life, these things surface; sometimes in physical illness, sometimes they form patterns of negative behaviour. Reiki allows a practitioner to tune into the client's energy field, drawing out the negative energy. Sometimes you need to talk about the past issue because often someone needs forgiveness. It may even be the client needs to forgive themselves, for being too hard on themselves. When I first practised Reiki, most people would have a nice calm experience; even if they cried, they always left feeling more content. One day, I was reading a book about self-healing; 'THE JOURNEY' by Brandon Bays. Then, a lady came to arrange a treatment. We arranged for the next day, I then continued reading the book. Brandon talks about going into a black hole, to deal with past emotions. I felt I already understood how we heal, but not about this black hole. During the treatment the next day, I felt I was swirling into this black

hole. If I had not read about this the previous day, I would have been terrified and would not have continued practicing Reiki. The lady having the treatment also sat up, saying she felt she was swirling into a black hole. I had not mentioned anything about this to her. I calmly asked that she lay back down and trust that Reiki is 100% pure loving energy; my intentions were in her best interest. Although she was scared, she did lay back down. The book gave me confidence to continue, knowing she would release any past issues. The session ended and she was absolutely fine. There are no two sessions, the same, with anyone and I didn't experience the same thing again. It is, almost always, about dealing with past emotions. We need to change the negative memory, then find something positive to replace it; when a new cell replaces the old cell, it will take on the positive memory. Brandon Bays describes this clearly, in 'The Journey'.
When you are attuned to Reiki, you are given these principles to say daily.

Just for TODAY, I will not worry. Just for TODAY, I will not be angry. Just for TODAY, I will be grateful. Just for TODAY, I will do my work honestly. Just for TODAY, I will show love and respect for every living thing.

I could never understand why we should say, *Just for today.* I wanted to live my life this way EVERYDAY. The Bible made this clear.

HEBREWS. 4. 6. There is another day TODAY (we should live in the moment)

Below is a client's experience of Reiki

JULIE BROOKS, EXPERIENCE WITH REIKI

Just over ten years ago, I met someone who would become one of my closest and dearest friends. I used to think meeting people who touched your life was just a coincidence. This person was to make me understand. We meet people for a reason. Special people enter our lives, not just by chance but because they are meant to come into our lives. There is a purpose, we cannot see at the time. I was going through a particularly low point in my life. I pulled up, to take a lady out for a driving lesson, it turned out I was to become extremely good friends with her. After spending much time with her, I realised we did not only meet so I could teach her to drive but because I had found someone who could help me through this low point. For a few years I had suffered with psoriasis and thought maybe she could help relieve me of this. Only later on, I realised she would help me with much more than this. I had been having tests, to find out if I could have children, these revealed I may have difficulty conceiving. Part of me had begun to realise, I may never have my own baby. After weekly sessions of Reiki from my friend, she said she thought I could be pregnant. The next day I went for a test, the nurse looked again at my notes and did two more tests. Her own words were, "Well, sometimes miracles happen." It was confirmed that I was pregnant. I now have a healthy, happy and love of my life miracle; my son, Will. I truly believe she gave me the strength, to believe in the power of positive thinking. I now live my life this way, believing a kind heart and positive attitude are the keys to a healthy, happy life.

I would like to add: when Julie told me about her condition, I told her that I could CURE her of psoriasis. Looking back, I feel I had a big ego. I could not clear Julie of psoriasis. From her first session, of Reiki, it was clear; the practitioner is not in control, we are channels. The energy has an intelligence, far beyond what we can ever imagine. It will flow to release blocked energy, which obviously was preventing Julie conceiving. I am thankful our friendship developed into a strong bond because she has been there to comfort me, so many times, since losing Claire.

Mathew…..8.16

Jesus drove out the evil spirits with a word and healed all who were sick.

Reiki is energy healing, so as Jesus cast out evil spirits to heal, a reiki practitioner draws out negative energy to heal.

(9)
Rachel's Story

(Rachel is my niece)

I always remember at the age of seven, waking up in the night and crying for my parents, over the fear of dying. This fear lingered over me for many years, all through my teenage years. Until I moved out of my family home, when I was eighteen, into my own flat. Whilst I was around people, and keeping myself occupied, the fear wasn't there. However, alone in my flat at night, a sudden panic would creep over me. What if I just dropped dead and there was nobody around to revive me? What if I blacked out and nobody was there to bring me back around? I would phone my mum, in tears, pleading for her to come through and sit with me. As long as I had somebody there, I felt reassured. To say it aloud sounds ridiculous, I know, but it was honestly the best feeling knowing that somebody was there to revive me if I stopped breathing for any reason. Obviously, this could not continue, I was getting myself into some real states when on my own. I was also calling on my mum, frantically, causing her to worry. It was one day when I was visiting Auntie Dawn, with my mum, that I told her about my fears; straight away, she suggested I have some reiki sessions with her. She knew fear inside was unhealthy and needed resolving. I had no real clue what to expect or what was going to happen. Just that, yeah why not I'll give it a go. I had several sessions of reiki, each one giving me a greater insight into my physical and spiritual body. I gained an understanding; how things that have happened throughout our lives, affect us in later life if not dealt with. During one particular session, I recall my mind being taken on a journey through my body in a capsule. I went back to the time of my first panic attack at seven-years-old. I'm unsure as to what triggered it at the time, but going back to that time through reiki gave me a relief from the fear and panic that had been consuming my emotions. The most significant part of all my sessions to me, was visualising strong, clear, clean air filling my lungs with every breath I took. This would then circulate around, deep inside me, and gather up a mass of black negative smog which would then be released from me as I exhaled. This is something I practice every day, as I believe it is filling me with positivity and clearing me of any negativity. Eventually, the reiki stopped and it wasn't until I was twenty-five that I realised how effective my previous sessions had been; how important understandings learnt, through reiki, are to us.

I was having a dressing changed at the doctor's, when the nurse asked me if I had ever had a smear test. She recommended I book myself in for one as I was twenty-five and a half, the age for your first smear. Due to becoming redundant from my employment a week previously, I had made an appointment. Had I have been working I know I would not have made the appointment. It would have been one of those things I would have eventually got around to in time. The smear test showed abnormal and so I was referred to a gynaecologist at the hospital. To this day, I still don't know why, but I attended the appointment alone and had no real worry or panic about it. It was as if I hadn't given the severity of the situation a thought. Literally, two minutes into the examination, the gynaecologist looked at me and said, "I'm 99.9% sure you have cervical cancer."

What? How could I? I'm twenty-five and had no symptoms or warnings, nothing. I was in complete shock, struggling to take in what he had said to me. I contacted my mum immediately, who came straight through to the hospital where I sat in tears. To be honest, I can't remember what happened after that. I just know when we were leaving my mum asked what I wanted to do, in terms of going home, telling people etc. An instinct told me I needed to go see Auntie Dawn. We went straight there and I just broke down and told her the news I had been told, not an hour before. She immediately reassured me, and my mum, that I would be totally fine and did I want to start some reiki sessions again. It had been a good five, possibly six, years since I had had reiki. I had faith in my auntie, though, and knew it would be beneficial.

Results came back, that the cancer was one of rarest of its kind. I was told, it was half a centimetre away from being incurable and the medical team involved were unsure of the best treatment. I started on chemotherapy, straight away, whilst the medics did more tests and put a care plan in place. It was agreed, I would have thirteen sessions of chemo alongside internal and external radiotherapy. Throughout all my treatment, appointments, tests and hospital stays I was having weekly sessions of reiki. Everything worked successfully in my favour, in that my tumour shrank and shrank till eventually, six months after treatment started, I was given the all-clear.

I, personally, cannot express how much reiki helped; not just in the process of me beating cancer, but in my understanding of how to live in a positive and healthy state. I believe so much, that the negativity that created the disease in me has been removed through the reiki I had. I was, and still am, filling my body with positive energy. Therefore the negative, in this case the cancer, had been pushed out. I have many stories to tell about the journey I took with cancer, but the most significant part is that I never let any negativity creep in. I didn't Google the disease or anything to do with it. I didn't read the leaflets given to me, of what symptoms I 'may' get. I didn't listen to stories of misfortune. I removed myself from sad aspects of life, such as depressing TV programmes, newspapers and idle gossip. Instead, I believed I was healthy. I knew, I just had a temporary blip in my health such like when we get a cold. I understood any symptom I got, was not to be given a second thought, as it was all just part of the plan to get rid of the disease. I watched lots of comedy and light-hearted programmes; I went on days out to have fun. I even volunteered, at my friend's school, to help out in the classroom and on trips (despite the tiredness and lack of hair, a fab wig helped with that). All this was taught to me, through reiki. It took me on a journey, teaching me that our words create and that illness stems from negative energy. We need to feed the positive and starve away the negative. I found ways to do this and I am extremely thankful to Auntie Dawn for showing me how to do this. There are many pitfalls to my life, from cancer, but I have never let them upset me in any way. If I did, I would be feeding that negative energy again. I understand that living, in the now, is key. What is happening, right at this very moment? When you think like that, you realise it's not all bad and that many things that stress/worry us are because we are not focusing on the now. I was told how my life would change through the treatment I received and did I still want to proceed? Err yeah, what other choice did I have? I didn't cry many tears with news that, at twenty-five I would be put through menopause or that there would be several medical issues that could occur later in my life (all treatable). One thing that I did get upset about though, was when I was told, "Yes, you will lose your hair!" My long thick blonde hair! My hair had always been my thing, I was distraught. After my first bout of chemo, I was told I would probably begin to lose my hair five weeks later. Nope. Five days later, on a day trip to Blackpool. My hair decided to start coming out in clumps. I gave energy to that negative aspect and look what happened. Fortunately, I had a gorgeous wig on standby, ready.

It wasn't till a while after I had received the all-clear that I realised, throughout the whole experience, not once, did I think about the thought of dying. It never crossed my mind once that this thing would take my life; that the treatment wouldn't work or that it would spread throughout my body (giving me five years of life, like I was told at one of my early appointments). There were no panic attacks, of what if this happens and I need someone to revive me. Considering how panicked, over death, I was in previous years; I was amazed to realise that this panic had not set in once. My previous reiki sessions had prepared me for this stage of my life. I needed to have that fear of dying to be able to overcome it; to be able to see my cancer through, with a positive, strong and determined attitude.

(10)
Our Thoughts and Words Create Our Situations

In 2007, a lovely friend, Mavis, gave me a Bible. Trev also got me the DVD of 'The Secret' and these were both life-changing for me. The first time I attempted to read the Bible, I just opened it randomly; it was like trying to read a foreign language, so I put it on my bookshelf. I then went on holiday; I met a lady who told me a fascinating story, about how she was ill. She was told she wouldn't make it through the night, but got a miraculous healing overnight through praying. She told me to open my Bible, at John, and all will make sense. I was in Dominican Republic, yet eager to get home and read my Bible. It was one of the first things I did when I got home. I opened it at John like she told me to. It said, "In the beginning was the word and the word is God." I kept saying this over in my head, it made sense to me. I closed the Bible thinking, *Where does this leave me and Trev?*

Trev's mum, at the age of about seventy, was hit by a car and suffered, before passing away. So he, myself (at the time) and many others thought, *How could God let something like this happen?*

I again, opened the Bible randomly; instead of going to the top left page, I was drawn to the right page (Peter 3). It basically says, your actions will be proof for your husband. O M G, the Bible answered my thoughts. 'The Secret' also says our words are creating what we experience. Basically, what we focus on, we create more of. I could see, by reflecting on my life, I had created so much misery myself. I was responsible for the situations I was attracting into my life, so I could now change my negative thoughts to positive. In 2007, I realised how destructive my thoughts were about myself. I would look in the mirror, thinking negative things about my hair and skin; so after watching 'The Secret' I knew I must be kinder to myself, by believing the affirmations I had already been saying. My face was now weighed down, with so much upset. A face-lift was not an option, so I really had to envision a more youthful vibrant me. How we feel when we say our affirmations, is important to what energy we attract. I am also learning to love myself, no matter what I see in my mirror.

My daily affirmation

I AM YOUTHFUL. I HAVE SOFT, HEALTHY, NOURISHED AND ENERGISED SKIN. I AM IN PERFECT HEALTH. THANK YOU, THANK YOU, THANK YOU.

Daily affirmation I say for Jemaine

I THANK YOU, JEMAINE'S FOOD HAS NOURISHED, ENERGISED AND REVITALISED HIS BODY. HE IS IN PERFECT HEALTH, HE CONTINUES

TO DEVELOP IN ALL AREAS. HE IS HAPPY, CALM, RELAXED AND CONTENT. HE CO-OPERATES IN A CARING WAY, WITH EVERYONE HE COMES INTO CONTACT WITH. JEMAINE IS A JOY TO BE AROUND. THANK YOU, THANK YOU, THANK YOU.

I had to smile to myself when Alison, a teacher holding a review for Jemaine, finished by saying, "JEMAINE IS A JOY TO BE AROUND."

Mark……..9.17
Jesus heals boy with epilepsy
Jeremiah. 46.11.
your medicine has proved useless; nothing can heal you,

Medication can relieve you, of something temporary. I have taken anti-histamines to ease my skin condition because I needed the instant relief. I would be a hypocrite, to tell someone not to take medication if they need some instant relief. We just need to have a plan, at some point, to deal with our issues; to prevent them surfacing as physical pain/ illness, later in life.

WHAT WE BELIEVE BECOMES OUR REALITY

After first watching 'The Secret', my husband, Trev, had just finished gardening. I sat, admiring our garden. I said, "I wish we had some bluebells." Within a few minutes, a woman came to our gate asking if we wanted some bluebell bulbs. O M G, I was experiencing the power of creating. How could this happen so quickly? Was this lady asking anyone? She lived about five houses away from me, I didn't know her. I had never spoken to her but found out after that Claire knew her. That doesn't explain why, almost immediately after my thought, she was there at my gate bringing what I had just wished for. Over the years, I have come to realise that some things come instantly, while other things we wish for may take some time to manifest. The reason for this is our belief; we think of all the reasons why we couldn't possibly afford these things, or even feel we don't deserve them. Therefore, we are basically blocking the original thought. What we should do is have a clear vision of it, then trust God/the universe that we will receive. If it's a perfect dress for a special occasion, the next time you shop, you could see it at a bargain price! You instantly know your energy created, you easily finding this at an affordable price. I've found clothes to be an easy one for me. I will put on a pair of trousers and see clearly in my mind, a top that would match perfect and I can almost feel the fabric. Because it has worked so many times, I am so sure I will see it. Because I now shop in charity shops, it is always affordable and also it always looks brand new. So now you are probably thinking, *Well, if you can manifest anything you want, why would you need to buy from charity shops?*

I don't need to, it is just my choice. I used to love buying new clothes; sometimes buying two of the same thing, just in case one got damaged. New or previously worn, makes no difference to me.

LAUREN'S STORY

Lauren is a friend, who practises positive thinking daily

FEEL YOUR WAY INTO THE FLOW ATTRACT WHAT YOU DESIRE

Anything we believe is possible. Nothing is out of reach.

A few years ago, my sister got a MacBook for her birthday from my parents; this was a very expensive gift. It was delivered four days before her birthday, and against my mum's wishes, she opened it. After the first day, she brought it to my house, my dog knocked a full cup of coffee over it. The MacBook sizzled and turned off. After the panic, we rang the manufacturer, who confirmed it was ruined. I refused to believe this and started to search for positive stories about water-damaged laptops. I found a few; they said to turn it off for three days. I immediately started attracting positivity. Each morning, for the next three days, I said thank you for this amazing birthday present. I would sit, looking at it, visualising my sister turning it on and using it. Finally, on her actual birthday, I wrapped it up and took it to her house; asking the universe for help. She unwrapped her present and laughed when I got her to turn it on. It was as perfect as the first time it was turned on and still works perfectly today. I had refused to believe what the manufacturers told me. Negativity doesn't bring anything helpful, we must always remain positive and thankful. We also found out that it is sugar that causes the damage; yes, there was sugar in the full cup of coffee.

Jemaine would copy other young people, who he came into regular contact with. There was a young person who carried lots of bags around, so Jemaine started to collect bags and fill them with anything he could; even getting annoyed because he wanted to fit more things into these already bulging bags. He had been doing this for about a year. One Sunday, he came home from York Villas Respite Care and did the usual routine; going to his room to get all these bags. He was taking cars apart, so he could get them into any spare space, almost breaking the zips. I kept going into his room trying to help him, then leaving his room and taking a deep breath, then going back in. He was frustrated, I was frustrated. Tuesday, I was taking him to York Villas so he went to get his bag. It then occurred to me that he hadn't had his bags all day, nor the day before. O M G I replayed Sunday in my mind, realising I had got so annoyed that I went to sit in my Reiki room to calm myself. I then remembered I had written something. I looked where I usually put my wishes, there wasn't a note there. I went outside, tipping the recycle paper bin out. Sure enough, I found a note. I had written, "Thank you, Jemaine no longer carries the bags about." The following Sunday, when we arrived home from York Villas, he went to his room to get the bags. I told him, "No, we don't have them now." He just accepted this, normally he would have just ignored what I said and just carried on doing whatever he was doing. To this day, he no longer has this obsession. When our wishes are answered we must always remember to say thank you.

NEGATIVE CREATING. It seems much easier than positive creating. I think it may be because we've been doing our creating unconsciously, for so long. For years, I have looked in the mirror; wishing I had silky soft hair, soft healthy youthful skin, what I saw was the opposite. Looking back at old photos, I didn't stand out any different from my friends. About four years ago, I started with itchy skin, it was then that I realised what I had been focusing on I had now created. I now had reason to not like what I saw in the mirror. But this is where it ends, I can't even write about it because I'm over it. I really can accept myself, we are all different, so I will focus on the things I am happy with. PLEASE, PLEASE, PLEASE take note, WE WILL CREATE WHAT WE FOCUS ON. In chapter five, I've wrote I needed to forgive someone, it was a few people including myself.

JEMAINE'S POSITIVE CREATING.

He goes to school with a school transport. The first part of term, he went in a silver minibus. He got me to take a photo of himself and his transport escort, Jayne, by the side of the silver minibus. After a few weeks, they changed buses to a black minibus. At first Jemaine didn't mind, then every time we went out in the car he directed me to where a silver minibus was usually parked up. He would say, "Jemaine, bus, home, Jayne." I would feel heavy with frustration, trying to explain, he couldn't just change minibuses. Every morning, while waiting for his bus, he would sit at the table with my phone looking at the picture of himself and Jayne, by the side of the silver minibus. He wouldn't plead with me, like when we were out in the car, he just sat quietly, patiently waiting for his bus. After a few weeks, he came home in the silver minibus. I asked Jayne why the different minibus she said, someone had crashed into them. Luckily no one was hurt. I don't believe he understands the laws of creating, but then he doesn't need to. He had just patiently sat each morning, focusing (probably unaware he was creating). Luckily my negativity (heaviness I had felt with it being something I couldn't sort for him) didn't block his positivity. WE REALLY DO HAVE TO BE CAREFUL WHAT WE WISH FOR.

BUDDHISTS saying.	WHEN THE HEART AND MIND CONNECT ANYTHING IS POSSIBLE.
BIBLE says MATTHEW. 17. 20.	WITH FAITH YOU CAN DO ANYTHING AT ALL.
HEBREWS.11.3	WHAT CAN BE SEEN WAS MADE FROM WHAT CANNOT BE SEEN.
PHILIPPIANS.4.6	ALWAYS ASK FOR WHAT YOU NEED WITH A THANKFUL HEART.
JUDE.20.	BUILD YOUR FAITH, BY PRAYING IN THE HOLY SPIRIT (THETA).

Below are different states of brain wave activity

BETA.	WAKING STATE
ALPHA	DAYDREAM STATE
THETA.	MEDITATION STATE

OUR HOME IS A GOOD INDICATOR OF THE STATE OF OUR MIND

If our home is cluttered we need to sort out things we no longer use, a cluttered house represents a cluttered mind. If you can't focus on things, then de-clutter. You will probably find excuses for not getting rid of things, especially if you're like me and love your clothes. But if you've not worn/ used it in the last twelve months, then get rid of it. It gives us an opportunity to have a good clean in those places we couldn't get to. This space in our home helps us have clearer thoughts. When I first started clearing out, I often got something back out of a charity bag only to put it in months later when I still hadn't worn it. The clothes we love are in excellent condition so let someone else enjoy wearing them. Not just for this reason, but when we let go of something, it allows something we need to come to us.

(11)
Self Help Techniques

WE SHOULD BE LIVING IN THE MOMENT, NOT THE PAST OR FUTURE

If life doesn't seem to be working for us anymore, we need to make some changes. We are constantly trying to get things done, so we can have time to enjoy life. We will never get everything done. It's about choice, when we choose to enjoy our time (obviously our work is important and certain jobs around the home) but we have to take time out. What you will notice, once you start to do this, is you seem to have more time. The reason this happens is because when we enjoy ourselves we are sending out signals of positive energy. These attract things on the same level of energy, directing to us more things / time to enjoy them. If this doesn't make much sense to you, best thing I can suggest is the next time you are invited to do something, but you feel you have too much to do, say YES. You will look back, maybe days later, realising the thing you would have done instead has either been done for you, or it seems clear to you that it isn't important anymore.

We need to become aware of our senses. When we wake each morning, we should try to be conscious of what we do. We are almost on autopilot. When you go to bed, if you can, put your alarm clock in a different place. When you wake up, you will be reminded why you've moved it. It is to become aware of everything you do. Feel your feet on the floor as you walk to the bathroom, feel the tap when you turn it on. Notice the smell of your soap, how soft the towel feels, etc. Usually, cleaning our teeth is one of the few things we actually focus fully on what we are doing. You should try to continue this throughout your day. It is only our thoughts, it isn't like it's something more we have to fit into our day. You'll be surprised, how you seem to have more time.

Lunch breaks are often taken rushing to do things, like grab some shopping for tea, etc., then eating our food in a rush to get back to work. We should sit and enjoy our food, tasting and chewing, being fully aware. Our thoughts, while eating should be on our food, believing we will be nourished by what we are eating. If you go on YouTube, Dr. Emoto (words on water) you will see an experiment showing the effects our words have on water. Just think about our body which consists of approx. 70% water.

I would get home from shopping, eating more food than I put in the fridge, not even really tasting or fully chewing it. I never put weight on so there was nothing stopping me doing this. But then I wouldn't put weight on because I was too busy dashing about catching up on things I believed had to be done. What a crazy way to live, but at the time, I wasn't even aware we could choose our thoughts. When I first realised I didn't have to think what my mind automatically thought, I was amazed I'd spent all my adult life letting my mind dominate me instead of me controlling my mind. I used to rush everywhere, complaining I've too much to do, this is what I created. My friends in similar situation as myself were not lazy. Their homes were clean, children cared for, but they weren't busy like me (busy getting nowhere). We can be NOWHERE or NOW HERE (in the present moment).

Take at least ten minutes, each day, to just sit in silence. Get comfortable, you could put some calming music on, maybe light a candle, or burn incense. Take three deep breaths, when breathing in imagine you're breathing in clear bright light when breathing out imagine breathing out sooty black smoke (all your negativity). If you can, become aware of your feet, ankles, shins, calves, knees, etc. Working up your body, when you get to your head, hopefully your mind will be quiet. If not, we now need to quieten our mind. At first, just allow your thoughts, which are usually trying to give you jobs, making you feel guilty for sitting doing nothing. So then say, in your mind, *I let these thoughts go.*

Try to imagine a feather, your thoughts resting on the feather. It floats up in the air and gently floats away, carrying your thoughts with it. If you are still struggling with thoughts, try counting backwards from 100, or start again at your feet becoming aware of each part of your body. Even if you don't go into a meditative state, you are practicing mind control.

We wouldn't have a few sessions in the gym and expect a perfectly toned body, but with regular exercise we can achieve our goal. It's the same with meditation keep practicing. For some strange reason, doing something physical, does seem easier than taking control of our own mind.

If you struggle with meditation, try going for a walk alone somewhere safe, where you can just focus fully on your surroundings. This is being mindful, any mind awareness is bringing you into a place where you will eventually have a peaceful mind whatever situation you're faced with.

We shouldn't dwell on past negative situations, we should use them to benefit our future. If past situations keep repeating, we must recognise what we need to change to prevent future reoccurrence.

(12)
Dreams

OUR DREAMS OFTEN HAVE HIDDEN MESSAGES

Bible. Numbers…12.6.
All will be revealed in visions and dreams

Bible. Daniel…....2.24.
Daniel interprets the king's dream

NOVEMBER / DECEMBER 2009. I had four dreams in one week; no dreams noted weeks before or weeks after.

FIRST DREAM, 30th Nov. My sister was cleaning dog and cat poo off her steps. MEANING: Stuck in a rut, needs to sort her S**T out.

SECOND DREAM, 1st DECEMBER 2009. I'm driving a double-decker bus up a straight hill, I eventually get to the top. MEANING: I've a real struggle ahead of me, but I will overcome it eventually.

Wasn't meant to know what my struggle would be. If my dream would have shown my daughter dying, I would have done anything to prevent this but this dream shows me it is all part of God's plan.

THIRD DREAM, 2nd DECEMBER 2009. My friend Trish was having her fiftieth birthday party; then we were at a celebration for Julie Hale (Rawson) my dream didn't show me what the celebration was. Julie is one of the nicest girls you could ever meet, this is said by everyone who knew her; sadly she passed away about eighteen years ago.

I felt I knew what my dream meant. There is a memorial by the side of the road, where Julie was hit by a car. I didn't know her birthday but wanted to check her headstone, to see her date of birth. Claire stopped the car, when we were going Christmas shopping, for me to look. It just said the date of her passing. I just assumed I was right and my dream meant it would have been Julie's fiftieth. I left it at that, only weeks later was I going to see the dream had much more of a meaning.

FOURTH DREAM, 5th DECEMBER 2009. Claire was in a helicopter hovering above her bed, (I've written in my diary) looking round sides of bed, doctor agreeing with her. MEANING: I found Claire lying on her bed; this dream means the helicopter represents Claire in spirit (fast vibration). We had no idea what had happened, so we were looking under and around her bed to see if there was anything to indicate what had happened. Because Claire was on medication, this is why I dreamt the part about the doctor agreeing with her, we wondered if she had taken too much medication (The correct amount of medication had been taken).

MEANING of my THIRD DREAM: One day I went to Claire's Castle (cemetery). I walked over to Julie Hale's resting place, it was then I realised my dream was not about Julie's fiftieth birthday. It was January 2010, ten years since Julie passed, so although it's not a celebration, every anniversary is a time to celebrate her life. I went to visit Julie's mum, reminding her I was a friend of Julie's, Julie's mum asked me if I was Brooky ? BROOKY IS TRISH the other girl in my dream. Julie's daughter had been touched by Brooky taking flowers every year and wanted to know who Brooky was. I was able to pass on Brooky's phone number.

Some meanings of common dreams

GOING UP A HILL	Facing a challenge. {It's a dream I have every so often when I'm faced with a challenge.}
GETTING TO THE TOP OF THE HILL	you will overcome the challenge
BEING NAKED	you are honest, you have nothing to hide
IF NAKED AND HIDING	you fear a secret may be made public
DEATH.	new beginnings
DOORS.	opportunities
IF DOORS ARE CLOSED	you've taken too much on

A dream I had of my Zumba teacher, Sara, holding a potato but offering a dessert. MEANING: She is offering to help us move from being heavy to light (although I will say, she encourages us to love ourselves the way we are).

So why don't we just dream the actual situation, instead of having to interpret our dreams? I don't know why other than, in the bible, Jesus talked in parables. Leaving us to work out the message he was giving us. It will help to keep our minds sharp, by working out for ourselves the meaning of our dreams. Also if it happens to be a death, (we would probably not see it has a new beginning,) I can't imagine how destructive this would be for us. We would want to spend every minute with this person. If we write our dreams down, its proof for us when it happens (unless negative, then dismiss these).

(13)
The Bible's Hidden Messages

This chapter is showing there is so much more to what we see, our words do have deeper often hidden meaning.

REVELATION within this word REVEAL ION
(The role of Ions in our body chemistry)

GOD + O = GOOD……. POSITIVE

DEVIL - D = EVIL…NEGATIVE

A NEGATIVE ION is known as an ANION
A POSITIVE ION is known as a CATION

If you think about a magnet
A positive attracts a NEGATIVE

An ANION has gained ELECTRON
therefore has a NEGATIVE CHARGE
so has a POSITIVE effect on our wellbeing

A CATION has lost an ELECTRON
therefore has a POSITIVE CHARGE
so has a NEGATIVE effect on our well being

NEURONS………………..	Basic information structure of our nervous system
SYNAPSE………………...	Small gap between neurons

Could our thoughts bridge the gap? Do our positive thoughts attract an ANION? Do our negative thoughts attract a CATION?

I found this a little confusing, at first; but if we think of walking into a room where someone has been arguing, this room now has positively charged energy. We wouldn't want to attract this into our aura. So the benefit of understanding energy, and how it affects us, are that we can now choose to leave this room; think a positive thought, to prevent automatically drawing in what is around us.

A positive thought is not the same as positively charged energy.

Many of us have constant negative thoughts running through our minds, could this be why we experience poor health and negative situations re-occurring.

GOD CREATED EVERYTHING, WE WOULDN'T RECOGNISE POSITIVE WITHOUT NEGATIVE

Bible........Ephesians.......1.10
God's plan to bring all creation together

Mark..9.29
boy with evil spirit, Jesus said, prayer is the answer to drive out this kind of spirit

REIKI
A Reiki practitioner goes into a state of meditation with a pure intention of releasing blocked negative energy

Revelation.13.18
666 is a man's name
If we turn these digits around we can spell 
Remember the Bible has hidden messages

GOD is both POSITIVE & NEGATIVE. We should turn any negative thoughts to positive thoughts

Bible...MATHEW.... 24. 29.

The coming of the son of man, Stars will fall from heaven, powers in space will be driven from their courses.

Jesus will rise again (son)

Scientists talk about the planets lining up with the sun. SON / SUN

DANIEL.......12.11.
time of the awful horror.
My interpretation (AWE FULL AURA)

HABAKKUK………………3.2

Splendour covers Heaven, we will watch in AWE my interpretation…sky full with AUROURA BOREALIS

NOAH………………God made a
RAINBOW, a sign of the covenant

When JESUS was born there
Was a STAR.
MATTHEW………..2
Star came up in the east

When Jesus was crucified there was an ECLIPSE

LUKE………………23.44
At about 12:00, noon, there was darkness

CHRISTMAS…..We overindulge on rich, sweet foods and alcohol.
EASTER………..(LENT) is an opportunity to fast. Detox, preparing for our skimpy summer wear
HARVEST………..fresh vegetable, fruit to nourish our bodies.

(14)
Words

Coincidences, hidden meanings and similar-sounding words.

The big question CREATION or EVOLUTION

Take away the same letters TION rearrange the other letters A CURE LOVE.

If we all treat each other with LOVE and respect, the whole world would be living in peace and harmony.

***

JOHN……..1.4 The word was the source of life.
The word is god.
WORD + L (HELL)
WORLD Do our negative words create our own hell?
Below are similar sounding words:

ADAM…………..ATOM
We are made up of tiny ATOMS.

EVE……………..EVOLUTION

We are gradually changing from five sensory to six sensory beings.

TOXINS………………..SINS

We do detox to remove TOXINS to cleanse our physical body.

We confess our SINS.

SILENCE………………..SCIENCE

We mediate silence to gain spirited knowledge.

We experiment to gain physical knowledge.

WELL…………………WE'LL
Together………………Mind, Body, Spirit
ILL……………………I'll
Alone…………………physical only
EGO…………………..I come……SELF
he go…………………GOD

PROPHET…………..PROFIT

A prophet gains spiritual knowledge.

We profit to gain financially.

DISCIPLE…………DISCIPLINE

Disciple gives up all to have a spirited life.

We discipline ourselves to achieve our goals.

NOEL…… No Hell

HISTORY... His Story

IMAGINATION... IMAGE A NATION
We use our imagination to create as god created.

INCURABLE...... Cure from within you can heal your life. (Quote by Louise L Hay)

MEDITATION...... MEDICATION

When we meditate, we are allowing our body to release negative emotions for long-term benefits.

My opinion, on anti-depressants and sleeping pills, is that we are here to experience life with all its ups and downs. So, while I would never tell anyone not to take them, I do feel it's our body's way of saying, "I am mentally drained, we need to take time out." I do believe our doctors have our best interest at heart, they know we want to keep going. These medications allow that; but at some point, whatever the issue was it will surface again. That's the intelligence working within us, wanting complete healing for us.

UNTIE.....Separate UNITE....Bring together

If we move one letter around, we have a different outcome; like with our lives. A simple change can make a big difference. Slow down, look to see if we can change anything, instead of same routine.

UNIVERSE
UNI…………..ONE
VERSE……….ALL TOGETHER

We all have an individual purpose,
but we are all working together as one.

EPHESIAN.1.10. All part of God's plan

ROMANS.12.5. Joined as one, but all have a different gift

THE LORD'S PRAYER	our father, who art in heaven hallowed be thy name thy kingdom come thy will be done on earth as it is in heaven give us this day our daily bread and forgive us our trespasses as we forgive those who trespass against us and lead us not into temptation but deliver us from evil for thine is the kingdom the power and the glory for ever and ever amen

If we say the lord's prayer, taking notice of the words, put these into practise, I believe we can have heaven on earth.

Daily bread	Is not just the bread we eat, but we need to feed ourselves spiritually.
Delivering us from evil	Releasing any negative thoughts without acting on them.
AMEN	It is so

THE GUIDE When a vision comes, provision follows

NEIL DONALD WALSH.........Everything we need we need
is within
If we don't go within,
we go without

CELESTINE PROPHECY It's the guidance within that leads us towards, a heaven that is already here, to know this is to know our destiny.

EVERY OBSTACLE WE FACE, GIVES US AN OPPORTUNITY TO LIFT OUR ENERGY.

IF WE GIVE ALL WE CAN, WE WILL RECEIVE ALL WE NEED.

SHOW LOVE, RECEIVE LOVE.

USE OUR PAST EXPERIENCES TO BENEFIT OUR FUTURE.

(15)
Bible Stories

FEEDING OF THE 5,000. Jesus fed the crowds, physically and spiritually. He gave them bread and fish, also he would have taught them to chew their food slowly and completely. We often swallow our food, after just chewing a few times, leaving more work for our digestive system. Notice the next time you eat a piece of bread, keep chewing until there is nothing left. You will find you are chewing far longer than you usually would be. Also, because you are totally focused on what you are doing, you will not eat more than your body needs.

MOSES, LEADING ISRAELITES TO FREEDOM THROUGH THE WILDERNESS PROMISED LAND. Our intuition is trying to guide us, but we are too busy or set in our ways to listen. So we are basically stuck in the wilderness. When we allow our intuition to guide us, we can become free of our addictions or the repetitive behaviour many of us are trapped in. Moving us into a more content life.

MARY ABOUT TO BE STONED FOR HER SINS. Jesus said, "Whoever has not sinned, can cast the first stone." Sin is anything we do but have a feeling we shouldn't be doing. We don't have to commit murder or steal; many of us sin against our own body. We should never judge anyone, no matter what they have done. Let their own conscience be their judge. Many act on impulse, or feel there is no way out of a situation other than to commit a crime. There is also many of us with addictive or obsessive behaviour; if we are told to stop doing these things, in our own best interest, we want those who advise us to mind their own business. So we should all focus on the best we can be, being kind to ourselves and everyone we come into contact with.

JESUS, TESTED IN THE DESERT FOR FORTY DAYS AND NIGHTS. Many make attempts to diet, stop smoking, whatever our weakness is. The reason it's so difficult, is because these things do give us a temporary good feeling which is usually followed by guilt. We are surrounded by temptation, no one but ourselves can make these changes. We have to make a conscious effort, see a result clear in our mind. A photo of yourself, from when you were happy with yourself, can help. Also, a daily affirmation. OUR WORDS DO HAVE POWER. We have to say it as if it has already happened; e.g. if food is the issue, each time you eat, become fully aware of the amount you are preparing. Saying in your mind, "Thank you for my healthy body, I am nourished and energised by my food." Then chew each mouthful completely and finish by saying, "Thank you." Throughout our day, we can help ourselves just by our thoughts. We can say, "Thank you, I am so content with my life", (even if we are not, we are creating what we want to happen, by believing this new understanding DOES work). Remember, Dr. Emoto's WORDS ON WATER: If our words have an effect on water and if our body is made of about 70% water, it's quite obvious that what we say about ourselves becomes our reality. Think over how many times you will have said, *I've got to lose some weight.*

You are creating the issue that you have got to lose weight. If you say, "THANK YOU, I AM MY IDEAL WEIGHT", you WILL create this.

We become tempted by bargains and special offers, even if it's something we don't need. I've seen so many children, under school age, get a toy in these £1 shops; simply because it's only a pound. Our houses become cluttered; more things for us to dust and clean. Less time to spend with our family, who know we love them because the plaques on the walls tells them, "MY FAMILY ARE THE MOST IMPORTANT THING IN MY LIFE." I'm not saying that our homes shouldn't be decorated with nice things; but if we're buying because it was cheap, that's the value it will mean to us in our home.

Here is an idea: the next time you pass a charity box, donate a pound. You will feel good about helping someone in need.

LUKE.10.40. STORY OF MARTHA AND MARY. Mary tends to Jesus' needs, then sits and listens to Jesus. Martha complains about how unfair it is; she is doing all the housework, while Mary just sits. If we all took some time, to listen to each other, there may not be as many of us who are stressed with being overworked. You may think, well then the work won't get done; you have nothing to lose by trying it for yourself.

JESUS WAS BETRAYED BY JUDAS, BUT THIS WAS ALREADY PART OF GODS PLAN.

LUKE.	22.3.	SATAN ENTERED JUDAS.
JOHN.	13.2.	THE DEVIL HAD PUT IN JUDAS' HEART THE THOUGHT TO BETRAY JESUS
EPHESIANS.	1.10.	ALL PART OF GOD'S PLAN TO BRING ALL CREATION TOGETHER

I believe that, before we are born, we are assigned a purpose. Sadly, for some, it is what we would consider negative or bad situations. However, we must remember that God created EVERYTHING; GOOD and BAD.

(16)
Short Poems Received Through Meditation

These short poems written by me, they come to me when I am dealing with difficult situations.
This poem came to me after Claire passed away

God said choose a mummy
Some teaching must be done
Your heart stood out from others
So I chose to be your son
You loved you taught
You cared for me
Nothing was too much
You smothered me with kisses
I miss your loving touch
God wanted you to join him
Your work on earth was done
You taught us unconditional love
You're missed by everyone
xxxxxxxxxxx

GUIDANCE AND COMFORT

I am your angel,
Always by your side
Whenever you need me
I'll be there to guide
When in times of trouble
All you have to do
Is tell me what your problem is
I'll help you see it through

FORGIVENESS

Forgiving isn't easy
And we never will forget
But forgive whoever does you wrong
Then you're not left with regret

***

LOVE IS giving, caring, loving and sharing

Give me a chance
To show how much I care
All I have I give to you
Which I trust you'll want to share

***

FRIENDSHIP

Whenever you're in need
I will always be there
To help in any way I can
Because I really care

***

Whenever I'm in need
I'm thankful you are there
You help in any way you can
Because you really care

***

HEALING

From my heart, which is pure
I send my love, this is your cure.

You may not cure someone just by sending your love, but you can put a smile on their face. We all need to make a good effort, to help someone feel better, by saying kind words.

When my children were young, my mother-in-law bought me a sewing machine. I had only ever made two things at school, under teachers' guidance. One of those was a tablecloth. Mary would buy some material, from a lady who made her own clothes, I could make the outfit quite easily. I would make dresses for Mary, Claire and myself, usually without a pattern. I often said, jokingly, "My machine talks to me."

If I was about to sew two pieces of fabric together, that shouldn't be sown together, it felt like someone was behind me; putting their hand on my right shoulder. So if ever I felt this pressure, I would stop and check that I was sewing the right pieces together. It was as though I had a teacher behind me, correcting me. Years later, when I went on a Reiki and Psychic awareness course, I was told we have spirit guides who work with us when we are doing something creative. So because I had not been taught how to make things, could that have been the hand on my shoulder?

THE BIBLE is a book that will find its way to you when you are ready. When I was given mine, I didn't feel ready, but within two to three weeks, I knew I needed to study daily. I read, a little, each morning. For me, it's a daily guide to help ease my journey through life.

BOOKS I RECOMMEND

LOUISE L HAY — YOU CAN HEAL YOUR LIFE
(we are all doing the best we can do with the knowledge we have at this time)

GARY ZUKAV	SOUL TO SOUL	
ECKART TOLLE	THE POWER OF NOW	
TARA BRACH	RADICAL ACCEPTANCE	
JOYCE MEYER	BATTLEFIELD OF THE MIND	
GOD CALLING	TWO LISTENERS	
RHONDA BYRNE	THE SECRET	also DVD
JAMES REDFIELD	CELESTINE PROPHECY	also DVD
NEIL DONALD WALSH	CONVERSATIONS WITH GOD	also DVD
ESHTER & JERRY HICKS	THE SECRET BEYOND THE SECRET	
SUPER SOUL SUNDAY	OPRAH WINFREY, A woman who lives her truth, speaks to spiritual guests.	
GILL EDWARDS	LIFE IS A GIFT	
DR WAYNE W DYER	THERE IS A SPIRITUAL SOLUTION TO EVERY PROBLEM	

If an object is broken, we can use tools to repair it. We can often restore it to its original condition. Many of us carry past hurt, this will eventually manifest as a physical condition, in a similar way we use tools to mend, counselling, gives us spiritual tools to help us with a different view of our past experiences, allowing us to see how forgiving someone will free yourself. If we become more loving, caring, giving, sharing we are restoring ourselves to our pure self as at birth.

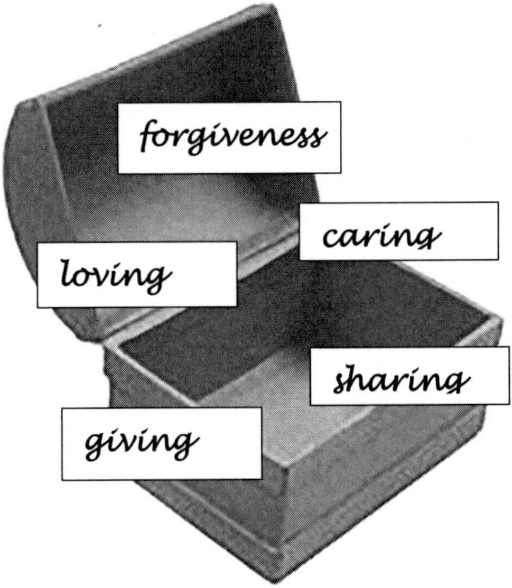